Life After Death, Death After Life

The Arrival, The Awakening, The Departure!

I0438225

By Raymoutez Price

DEDICATION

Dedicated to all my family who I learned from, some taught me to stay loyal and be tough. When the rough get going! This is in compliance to my family near, even distant, I always think of you all! I inspire you all to be together always! Never let a stranger violate your family lines with deceit stay together never separate, remember from the big house till death! Family first, God number one. The World is last and protect yourself, your love ones by all means necessary! If society fails you, stay strong as family and don't fail each other! Don't be afraid fight to the last string, the last man, women, and child.

Strength is in numbers and Ink is power with under standing, knowledge and the ability to protect yourselves and family in a 200 miles radius! Always think before you thought! Know and trust in no-one outside family! The most important weapon is your ability to know one another, be prepared in days when changes occur! Watch the people in the hills and if they run or get well prepared don't cancel your selves out as victims! If you are ready you ain't gotta get ready! I learned that people can turn to the way of the world and money is power but if used wrong it is a sickening corruption!

Remembering God is the true Savior, He help those who help themselves! To: R-Coleman, W-Terrel, D-Greenfield, C-Greenfield, R-Jones, M-Jones and cousins N-Hendrix, G-Wilbert, T-Wilbert, V-Wilbert, N-Wilbert, L-Coleman, J-Coleman, Lil Ronnie, N-Coleman, K-Jones and all the few soldiers counted on two hands who are loyal and stay loyal to the loyal!

REST IN PEACE: Tyshawn Wilbert, Barbara Adams, Marquis Wilbert, Ernest Covington, Eurudell Wilbert, Vindera Wilbert, Shirley Covington, Demetrius Coleman, Terry Coleman, Maxine Jones-Price, Ronnie Coleman, Bonnie Sue, and all the existing unknown family in our family tree who may be unsung heroes and also the friends I grew up with and learned from R.I.P.

Life After Death, Death After Life

The Arrival, The Awakening, The Departure!

Written By
Raymoutez Price

Photos By
Raymoutez Price
Quotesvalley.com

LIFE AFTER DEATH, DEATH AFTER LIFE:
"The Arrival, The Awakening, The Departure"
Copyright © 2014, Raymoutez Price
All Rights Reserved.

Author Contact Info
Raymoutez Price
razmatazprice@gmail.com
www.razmatezprice.com

Self-Publishing Associate
www.BePublished.Org
Commercial Ave. – Chicago, IL
Dr. Mary M. Jefferson
P.O. Box 8324
Jackson, MS 39284
mari@bepublished.org
972-880-8316

Imprint of Record
CreateSpace dba On-Demand Publishing
7290-B Investment Drive
Charleston, SC 29418

First Edition
Printed in the United States of America.
Recycled Paper Encouraged.

TABLE OF CONTENTS

<u>Chapter I</u>

Sleep-Walkers & Unknown Flying Objects

I awoke in death, I was dead in life! I lived re-incarnated, Although I walked amongst the living and dead, very few people were like me, whom were trapped in the matrix in between, in limbo unseen or unknown worlds were visual to mankind. The thought of many lies told with religion. While living throughout many past lives, some which brief flashes created an spontaneous de'javu people whom seem so familiar, a lure or energetic pulling of two positives combined with negatives canceling out or permitting the Edition of things or events of occurrences. To become realities or non realities of things subtracted and loss as erased memories, which becomes flashes of neurological blemishes of an event that vanished. Although resignation in small amounts of traces which allowed a spare given gift of foretell or prophesy to prevent failure or casualty in prior existing lives in which remembering is putting puzzle pieces together.

Reshaping failure into accomplishments of success, overcoming the essence of premonition, repentance. Divine intervention brings certain people closer, reigniting, allowing a similar past to become a recreation of past events. Which only the law of limitation as destiny causes near brushes of death or life. Prevention with divinity depending on Angelic decisions, allowing the final calls of let live, let die. During intense moments when brushes with death are many. Although 1 in 9 billion people you are in a stand still moment as time has paused. As if infinity was forever, time passed slowly as your life was being displayed on a venue or platter revealing the likes of divine intervention, playing itself out in a way of freedom and pure expression which your memory blossoms unlike anything you had ever witnessed before. Somehow you were inspired to focus on being spared an holy divine intervention occurred resulting in prevention as you question yourself asking why me? While 9 billion people live and die!

7

Although during your brief brush with the unknown, unforeseen realm of death. Which happens to disregard you at the very last second, it was not your time something happen which a voice says, Let him live, the darkness soon becomes very intense, trying to pull you back without loosing another soul to the light. The deep emotions get angered and death tends to put a mark on your life. So that in life or death, it shall always have an beacon of location of your whereabouts! Because you have cheated death, it seems to be enraged with you always attempting to cause you some sort of inhumane malfunction or uncertain demise of final destination, of some sort! In a figure of speech, a monkey wrench tossed in the Game. Attempting to claim your soul, although rather your claimed or totally lost, depends on your efforts there after your brush with death. Scrutinized with all sorts of bodily invasions of sicknesses and disease as some sort of message of revenge and payback results of the savior within, the bright lights which pulls you similar to gravity and reshaping, the being according to his very own will to prevent casualties of self inflicting condemnation, of one own deeds of moralities carried out, inflicted upon ones own neighbor, which it is translated "Live bye the sword (gun), die bye the sword (gun)! Spare and you shall be spared! Live and let live!

Somehow when two lost people whom had lived a life together, once before, one thing pulls them together out of pure coincidence. May be an old fire which lingered briefly! Deep within a realm, we were not familiar with the glimpse to allow us sight or touch. Which could have lasted seconds, although for an divine uncertainty, in which we are unaware as human. A realm opens reuniting the re-acquaintance of two people whom were once consolidated, considered as one whole as an couple, within another existing realm where two people shared life or a common goal of living and enjoying, loving one another being deeply in love. In death sharing becomes a reality of other realms in which ordain gifts from heaven is granted guaranteed to anoint peace beyond, somehow souls and spirits happen to reunite intertwining, reliving the best times or moments of past recreating presents which had been lived and some had been filtered out with very minimum memory.

Being human one has no recollection of the past events that exist of a prior life existence, previous lives events are that much more distorted, unfamiliar with his short term memory, simple human thought three percentage usage of the brain power allowed to be used or manipulated as abnormal, although with death realms open. Which was impossible or prohibited unknown in life is now visible, now limits reaches beyond the heavens and places, called Galaxies and being restricted becomes unlimited and out of touch, becomes that which is unimaginable! Coming to an beginning end, within the second death of the soul. Filled with indulging trauma, which becomes difficult to understand, although the feeling is detrimental to life and knowing pane is knowing existence is realistic. Theological to theory with true belief of miracles occurring and prayers that are answered! Seeing with a sub-countenance thought with-in allowing your inner light to shine bright, transcending with traveling out of the body experiences with meditation of tapping into ones inner strength and mental state of comprehension of knowledge. Of coarse one must have inclined accomplished pure Grace in order to be considered chosen as permitted.

I became shackled of my slave thought, my deeds canceled out by my own emotions, defeating myself time and time again. I learned how to settle all thoughts, allowing and practicing how to control my emotion and especially my uncontrollable rage and anger... I talked to my father above! The both sides revealed it's domains, that which is high even that which is very low. I developed great knowledge from above and beyond, with the emergence of knowing. I assumed the most important thought and action which was to proclaim secrecy covertly undermining the value of the realistic truth, which may have permitted and qualified me as mentally disturb in the human man made world of design laws of limitation. Amongst silly mortals upon releasing my untold truths, I would be declared and stigmatized written off as an very intellectual individual with very outstanding peculiar views of concepts relating to the normal way of mankind, sort to speak seemingly, different mostly rare breed then most sticking out as to say similar to an soar thumb! Which certain people with a very keen eye notices the big differences of

9

an rare creation! As to say or compare an Albino born human whom is Physical defined as different. As a genetic human specimen, due to very rare genetic traits changes manifest as abnormal. Although countenance and soul is considered different with obscene viewing and very low contraceptive of perception of liberated freedom of procreation divided separately internally or interior from the human flesh! Almost similar to an Pistachio or breaking an egg-shell open to retrieve the yolk! Which the creation within exist some one of very rare traits, the means of carrying out deeds, which may happen to blossom soon or even later imprinting an prestigious effects on world kind in a manner which is divine with a purpose of reliving a previous purpose in life.

Creating a purpose of existence preventing a full scale event, life of wasted blank unfilled pages. The worlds of spiritually. I come from places far away from this place, which makes one Alien or considered not belonging to the word called Earthlings or the species in which human exist. Being Alien is just a state of thought or state of living and existing in state of mind, or place where unfamiliar terrain is manifested as unknown!

Within I begin to study deeply, meditating, forever growing evolving finding the true me, manifested so many layers in my own thought, even within others around me, whom played significant roles in my previous journeys. We have been brothers/sisters through-out time, some genetic defective seeds which have traces of, the ones whom are with-out spoil. The last of a kingsmen-ship breed pure untouched perfect in stature.

The ability from one man to many gifted. One life sustains until a trace of the old-man hidden with-in the cave erected himself up-ward, walking bent over due to the lack of pigmentation his skin transformed into a form of disease. He had no color he was a different type of being evolving different from the first man created. Defects in his blood distinguished him distorted and rare as to be one out of 9 billion.

Chapter II

What Was Leprocy?
A Curse Or Skin Disease,
Or Simply A New Race?

The Sun-Rays could kill this man if exposed extremely to long his very rare genetic traits, were considered to be an mutation amongst normal humans, as the skin seem to turn as to say albino lighter then most of humankind. It was considered to be a plague. Which most people whom were considered to be with this disease, they were excommunicated and exiled. They hid themselves in strange places such as within the Jungles or any such place where human life didn't exist. Their most peaceful place was with-in the Earth core. Sometimes these plagued people were hunted and tormented for being different as this so called disease claimed many lives. Although it only distorted the appearance of skin color and pigmentation, had decreased it became genetic, children were born completely opposite of the original coloration of mankind and a disease called leprosy became that which is known as race an brand new tribe was born to the very first infected person whom had become a victim to leprosy. While living in caves where the sun was limited to shine, his skin became much lighter. Millions of years passed in the time once during the years so far long ago the change was inevitable!

"The Great Arrival" occurred the awakening and departure was imminent. He ran being led inside the Earth to be protected because few were different. Mercy had been found in the few that were good, through time the evil of animalistic traits surfaces in the genes, skipping certain generations defecting certain births. The Women intermingled with the first man who had been created to endure sun-rays, so-on, so forth pro-creation occurred to splice the two creating a mixed Man or Women child born of different groups . Whom seed spread through out world-kind. Thus developing two different types of species one with a pure blood-line and every-one else. The Man the infected one with leprosy and everyone else with this so called disease of lighter skin pigmentation came from him, whom had been born different, he lived only assuming he was sick because he had a disease that effected his skin, he appear much lighter, while certain skin spots were brown in some areas, although white mostly all over! Some births occurred where the children entire bodies were considered a plagued.

    After thousands of years passing, they begin to call a plague race majority, they populated and conquered many lands as they were promised through God after their punishment of being last and suffering abuse of a castaway. They became first conquering lands. They spread across the land from the seed of first man created, in the image of the star-beings different oppose to the very first creation. Although life arrived from the heavens above, all humans are a product of he that dwells from above. Existence from their seed, so forth all men of color and without color would evolve through-out time. Creating his-story to be told. Setting forth the law of order the wright-away of passage into this world. The plan had been put in place to protect the purest rare seeds, from becoming mixed, crossed breeds in this experiment to recreate the first beings. Whom destroyed themselves in flesh, leaving behind their residents of spirits without form.

    They were created from above protecting the order, the terrain far from the physical world which were dimension only the spiritually inclined were permitted to travel. They returned incarnated in the flesh. Awakening World-kind how our pass destruction, effected future, not repeating failed History! Wars separated many which an hate and created imbalance of destruction plague most of the visitors from long ago whom had traveled and became disbarred to travel, to the foreseen sights above, due to some very stealthy committed crimes. They were charged and indicted to serve an existence in a place that is foreign! Although it was a very critical and overwhelming punishment, they prospered turned a punishment into a blessing! Of coarse I'm referring to those whom were blessed to receive the least less harmful sentences, in which they were able to redeem their names for goodness sake, return punishments served, and commune once again with the way of the Galactic inter phases of Supernatural Curriculum.

They now watch! Monitoring our every move, knowing every advantage and disadvantages of the human flesh. The way we desire, love, hate, live, survive, with will, how we endure extreme physical pane, death. Some people whom are miserable, although they need or want attention. Company mistaken as friends whom you should flee far away from, such diseased prone, preposterous friends. After once living, they have been around longer than thought itself! With great intelligence and creation of technology, they can never be captured by world-kind! Creating more war! We need them more than they need us living in flesh. They keep us in spirit! We are inclined to find the correct path, which leads to the promised forbidden realms of forever. We must become pure traveling through the natural order of the Universe. In-order to transcend into our previous state of mind! Peace within our purpose along this journey is to find the natural effects of feelings inside control of emotions which cause men to become tainted in the flesh. Snared by gravity tapping into a old belief of cosmic energy source called aura. Which surrounds the human flesh, with different sorts of energies which are Inter-dimensionally, positive energy, the most strongest pushing forward life in evolution. The reminisce of pass creations (The Universe).

The Earth is living breathing, The Earth is the mother to all world-kind! We are her offspring from before when she was in another home, even she changes with moods. The use of weather in locations abroad, to keep herself restored, she brings forth life in abundance. She protects her dead, she takes them with in her as their lives expires, she protects their essence in other forms of life around her allowing them to blossom like a rose-bud!

She is made of many element's, she has many plains water, land, soil, mountains, skies, volcanoes, swamps, seas every place producing forth life, clouds which have different types of layers or purpose with-in layers performing many great task, which compliments the duties of every other element, example clouds, dark clouds, misty clouds, sunny clouds, steady clouds, twirling clouds. The sun, bright sun, early sun, noon, evening sun, low sun, high-sun. Water, tsunami. Tidal waves, calmed waves, rippling waves, above water, deep-blue water, river water, lake water. Drinkable, sustainable water. The earth consist of many things from gases, fluids, flesh, life of all sorts and she is the keeper of all things for she is so beautiful within her beauty, from above seen from the heavens, she yields forth beauty. The seeds that are un-pure which is mentioned by Jesus! Unclean spirits. They seek to end her corrupting pure seed's here. They have no good intentions. I do not know why they intend to set destruction across the planet Earth. With attempts to become a destroyer of planets. They have created ways to lower her defense and ole zone layers in attempts to breach a jail sentence. The fallen seek to reenter the above far beyond. Mechanism are created given as gift to test our sternness and maturities. In order to straddle the atmosphere traveling pass the four flaming swords, of the four corners of the Earth, beyond the heaven's to protect her against foreign and domestic invaders.

Which want to pluck or drain her, for she has many elements desired. Her co-ordinance has been hidden for many eons. The disagreeable arrives, wars will manifest on Earth, for they will seek to conquer pillaging the villages for all things that exist! Many forms which we call Aliens beings are Angelic beings protecting us in unseen invisible to the necked UN-couteance human-mind of sight!

This war is biblical, it has existed for billions of years. The evidence is in our history books. Bibles, landmarks, such as Pyramids. The ying-yang theory exist, far beyond humans natural know it. These Super natural beings have many functions, some are in spirit form as the human flesh to deliver a pure message to prepare the people during the process of enlightenment. The message get's distorted it has been found that in stone ingravement such as hieroglyphic writings on stone tablets or inside of caves, proven to outlast the destruction of nature and time.

It's the one and only written proof which can-not be distorted are deceptively re-written eradicated or erased in-order to manipulate the message, if they can not distort the message, history has proof re-arrange, disfigured words or appearances of

14

the Sphinx broad wide nose. Seeking to distort such knowledge. These evil forces have gone out their way to destroy the entire stone, eradicating all proof of truth and existence! Although many places were spread out World wide containing the same truth. The story was most imminent to stay the same to indicate the resilience in a plan of galactic purpose! Once it was discovered the similarities were highlighted being one in the same regardless of how hard the opposing forces tried to erase the moral existence of the true messages, that lay hidden worldwide.

Some forbidden places, have yet to be found because the elements of time is not exact and alignments and coordinates are not yet set to intertwine with time that is set forward. When the last bit of information is revealed, the star children shall arise no-matter what! Wordwide to perform great unbelievable task, creations of existences defeating the opposing forces of war and greed!

Chapter III

The Watchers And The Chosen

The Awakening is manifesting of the world, finding out the hidden truths, being self aware of many layers, Vampires and leeches that come here, are very upset that their food supply is becoming rebellious refusing to be subjects or meet suits to any foreign unclean vulgar vikings, invading their vessels, using them for lunch and satisfactory purposes. We have the wright to forbid being touched or violated by any-one, physical or non-physical. God sent here on earth with a purpose is Angelic beings, with righteousness and respect for all things, for the creator of just purpose and cause which remain benevolent to righteousness, what we have been taught for eons avoid the deceptiveness of the unseen and the unclean spirits! Whom have not any respect or concern of teaching the sleepers cells. Awaking un-countenance how to develop awareness. They are not the ones here that want you to awake, they have a better interest of keeping you docile, deceived in distorted beliefs, so that you are in a deep slumber. They continue to feed off of your genetics creating cloned like beings and slaves to cater to them!

Misleading more pure blooded humans into the slaughter house of doom! In order to steal their star light, soul! We must awake fight back help those whom help us! It has been many Women and Men whom have seen the values of this beast that lingers inside the flesh of world-kind! Taking advantage of the animals alike! When your in-tuned with the earth you become one with the earth! Understanding the animals, the plants the trees all communications, they are not happy for crimes are against us all. Animals are stronger smarter than most humans think! We call people with the lack of intelligence fools or bird brains, in true reality we are the true bird brains! We call animals that are suppose to be below the food chain bird brains) or food. We sit at the very top of the pile as rulers? Take-away the weapons, move back into the Jungles, then we are placed to live next to the lions, hyenas, wolves, bears! Whom would become the eaten the prey or the predator? We have lived like this once before, not many of us succeeded, so we moved far away into areas void of beast. Whom fed on humans. We moved to parts of land, where small animals resided. Our bully instincts consumed us while we turned them into foods. Although the animals that ate us, We feared, we wouldn't consume their flesh in our same weakness, if we are stronger than an opponent. We seek out to inflict and oppress them in our own weakness! We are not strong around the strong, but yet we are weak when we are strong in front of the weak! The strong is strong in the mere presence of the strong!

Tyrants trample weaker countries. Although smaller countries are stronger than the tyranny possessed by the oppressors. How foolish is man or a bird-brain, when so many of our Caucasian brothers wonder off into the woods and they stumble across the dumbfounded bird-brain mountain-lion? Which devours the human flesh defecates the remains in the woods. Humans becomes a part of photosynthesis and plant life, the same applies for the Bears, the crocodiles whom are suppose to be one of the dumbest animals alive. Now if he is so brainless, why does it make man lunch meat? On their very broad diverse menu? Is mankind considered smarter than the average bear? Or is he compared to a bird-brain? Is he on-top of the food chain or the bottom? If you are on-top, why are you available for dinner? You have to be a full participant in-order to give yourself that title, you have to wrestle defeat the bear, the lion with-out gun or weapon then you are truly (King of the Jungle)!

White-men traveled to Africa, they knew of lions although they had never seen a beast of great magnitude and agility, tamed to walk next to a man, domesticated as pet, they witnessed the Indians tame Wolves and Grizzly Bears, how they walked with Bears and Wolves! They studied Ancient Tribes discovering their true secrets and self-proclaimed the white-race the first and foremost dominant race! They had discovered the principals of taming beast, thus they went out their ways to domesticate the beast, with violence and tyranny, which animals felt the tyranny of white-men and his hatred inside grows strong to eat all humans in general!

They loose their trust, notice how crimes against them are permitted, domestication, ways in which destroys their existences. What animal dreams born created destined to riding bikes? Interrupting the natural order jumping through scorching flaming loop's tampering with our Wild Kingdom? Interrupting the natural order of Gods design for animals? Who do Animals attack after Animals attack? Every Tiger, Lion, Elephant, Crocodile, Great Silver Back Ape, Grizzly and Pole Bear have attacked humans after being effected psychologically and mentally! Lost habitats and misplaced as captured side shows of entertainment. The captures feed them and assume he is happy... After taking him out for a brief walk, if you don't understand why he wants to eat you? Try this! Place your self in the most dangerous Prison known to mankind then wait to see how dangerous the animals are once you let them out of cages? And you are the one who put them there!

The Earth, the people have been violating natural order of earth which have been interrupted. People are participates of experiments along with animals considered subjects, joined as one in torment. The voiceless cry-out, when man tries to become Gods, they forget they are not immortal with lives. They can feel, touch, just like their experiments or subjects, if you can be touch or live, breath as a man? If you can reach-out in a gesture to shake hands, you can be eliminated. The natural order always realigns itself by destroying the one who disturbed the order or peace, which is once again restored. This is called Karma. One of the reasons mother Earth is abruptly explosive, cleansing itself of so many disruptive seeds, become germs without any concern, about her feelings of needs. Anger is felt world-wide reaching a boiling point. We run hide from wrath as anger is unleashed, mankind can't hide any place. There is no place which is safe from disaster.

The Watcher's have been around longer before we were! They follow a natural order, everything works together, Ying Yang when a renegade is off limits or boundaries. He is observed captured, confined, until judgment. Punishment has been instructed that has always been the way violation of the human flesh is forbidden. Our planet has been set to go into a stage of realignment, doors open passage occurs. The Watchers wait to restore them back once it has passed over. The Police of the Spirit world of righteousness are ordained by the creators of the Universe! Along with great powers begets great responsibilities! Outlaws whom have been subdue attempts these jail-breaks, they have no remorse they violate human flesh seeking emotional-pleasures or desire's! Which binds the human flesh, creating negative thoughts in the sub-thoughtfulness mind of men. Unleashing floodgates for others creating much work for our protectors.

Do they have voices? In the olden days Men talked with God! Alone, some Men were Representative of God sent in Angelic form! Visiting Men that were compatible with, becoming one and other times they were in your Aura. The energy around your vessel protecting you from any thing unclean. Super Natural beings, have been assigned duties to watch over us in our slumbering! Guarding our ancient spirits, that are vulnerable in our deep sleep. They watch over us welcome us once our journey has been completed. We all must live die. Going through this transformation choosing sides. The Ying or the Yang, we are not aloud to be touched until our time has arrived, our clock is completed. We have learned to reach our pivotal point. Which we have obtained our paths desires, thirst have become exhausted experiencing death! The hurting dreadful feeling of being alone forgotten keeps us in our journeys, until we find our rightful place.

Chapter IV

Never Ending Divine, Cosmic Love
That Doesn't Expire

We move forward, we are searching for family, we have losses, our love is so strong that we can find each other in death! Although you must have a natural true bond called love, or you will never find your true love! You will lose purpose destination. Love that is true, you can separate the two even in different Galaxies or Milky ways you can find your true loved ones.

Love is a cosmic energy, like a magnetic pulse, a rapid heart-beat, just with-out the heart, the true feelings of love inseminates through your brain-waves creating thought and human emotions, that pulls and lures attracting your related love ones, back to you even in dreams you can be set apart. Restore your existence as one bonded together, spiritually in-tuned with husband and wife. Love is one of the greatest feelings in the world! It is compared to joy, happiness and pleasure of enjoying a companion when the two love-birds/mates make love, like two strings intertwined as one in ecstasy overwhelms the flesh. Thoughts ravel together the ecstasy of colors form in your brains, the dopamine is releasing enormous amounts of pleasure, now if he or she has been incarnated.

You have been together thousands times before, it is that much better when the juices flow inside, you take it slow, feeling each-others heart-beat combine as one consolidated pulse, joined in a ceremony of love, joy, affection, you opened up invited with out violating. This women she gives you her precious, divine, virginity. She has been treating her-self accordingly holding on to her pureness and virginity until the perfect match or soul-mate was sent from heaven above! Restraining not to become like the masses, number of Women following the stereo-type wanting to be equal losing herself and soul in the process, chasing fantasies of straightening their kinked hair for the allure of being accepted as beautiful!

Feeling wanted and accepted with long straight Caucasian

hair, falling for sexual publicity stunts by the worlds deception. Teaching young girls that Women can choose to sleep around with men & women, degrading one-self while being brain-washed, to show-case their necked flesh and it's okay! They are being used as a sex symbols and objects of pleasure in this deceitful perverted demonic persuasive way that is considered harmless and justified. Although truth is any tool used to get Men & Women to drool and lust from their mouths watching a half-necked Women/Men on the front cover of a magazine! It's just a plain out a tool of evil designed plan to keep Men/Women as Prey. In this hunt which we are confused who's hunting, while with truth we are just afraid to say who is hunting us!

Hearts are unproved, constantly lusting, for human desires, entrapping themselves with the help of media and entertainment. Fully co-operating in this massive plan of modern day legalized genocide. Very few Women are remaining old fashioned, with the old kindred spirit keeping one self pure with Morales, dignity, pride, and virtues. Most of all self-respected.

So the art of love making becomes that much more valuable. Pure in it's essence, rewarding her Man whom She has chosen as her partner a life time mate forever. It is a spiritual desert, a treasure that creates pleasure in the mind felt through-out the body. Some people might be ashamed to speak about such a topic those whom are inclined in the essence of true love and destiny. There are black demon beast in the African American race, period and all they think is pure evil daily. Some of them go to Church on Sunday praising Jesus calling themselves true Christians. They hit the clubs searching for sexual partners. Taking them home to screw like caged animals.

The next day they act as if they hadn't met, never to speak again! This my friend is the life-style, the new millenniums way of making love, you don't make love! you just are having sex! Partner's in friction and collision. The word love is almost forbidden! Until it happens then the complaints are always he don't love me! She don't love me! Love wasn't the way it started! It most definitely isn't how it will end. They chose to engulf in lust, until emotions got raveled confusing lust with love, A crave a burning desire feeling in the world that many Men will not pass up or refuse. We always victimize each-other!

Why does black on black crime exist? The truth ladies and gentle -men is because we been betraying each-other forever, some Men and Women rather be having lust! Rather then having love made to them! In it's purest form of-coarse opposite genders apply in the purest form of sexual conduct! Homosexuality by all means are unpure unjust forbidden, illegal, wrong. It is written, it is a fact! You know it's in the book called Bible "God created from the wound of Man a Women" for Man to be joined and become one as a couple Husband and Wife. Men and Women who live like animals want to destroy the Husband/Wife agendas so they can act like caged wild beast having orgies like dogs! Sleeping around engaging in open relationships, spreading diseases misinforming the young girls that watch. A lust for animalistic sex is developed in the minds of the youth, passed down as a cruel gift of knowledge, they grow-up thinking this is love being beat and having make-up sex. A Ghetto mentality a Jerry Springer dialogue manifesting in the girls that will become Women creating a rift between true Women hood and becoming more like Men-whores.

Never experiencing true love or soul-mates, after having so many different sex partners the value and appreciation for sex decreases, Men and Women are considered on a scale ratio rated for the quality of sex comparing numbers, like dice rolling craps then once in a while a seven and eleven. The old ceremony of pureness and divinity in-which two virgins waited until marriage. Where it became sacred they both were knew to this and had to learn the truth of love-making, experiencing the pleasure together learning everything about sexual body anonymity together. Making mistakes laughing and correcting it. The first time together with your soul-mate is exciting, exuberant exhilarating, scary overwhelming, feeling special nervous for the very first time you will share love with some one special un-like some booty-call! When you get laid you get paid! You forget in seconds what happened.

Sex that is manifested pure and by law of Gods order, last for a life time. The memories never fade away! Women have been violating themselves allowing the world to get away with it publicly. Especially for the Women who walks into a slaughter house, eyes wide open. She only gets what she desire's to be a door knob, giving every one a turn letting every man walk on her as a carpet. Playing the role as a robot or sex-slave rolling over, barking, farting, demoralizing her sexual-gender with sleeping with other Women. No-man will have respect for Women that don't respect herself first and for-most! If you have a son when he finds out his Mother is a whore the first Women he ever loved, he will develop hate becoming a womanizer also he will search for love by relations with other race ethnicity searching for that which he wasn't taught that exist in Women after observing his own mother being effected to a slave mindedness and lure to prostitute herself and the precious temple as if she was a piece of trashed to toss and be thrown away.

Boys whom witness this usually disrespect the Women of their race. When a black Man usually only deal with other races and he excludes Black Women, it is because he have witness unspeakable acts performed without any respect toward him as an child, as he grew and learned the differences of want whores were, while his friends were so called player macking to whores, he became embarrassed to know that how his friends treating whores sharing and tossing her as they all took turns. A whore would have sex with over ten friends as the boy witness this, a loss of respect for his mother grows as she introduce her next trick male friend to her son. He grows enrage thinking of all the years and all the Men he have seen routing in and out of her home dating, all the exotic loud animal noises she made while he attempted to get rest.

He begin to think all Black Women were whores or Gold-diggers! He established an self appointed distrust and label of disrespect for all Black Women, first he Identified them as mother Secondly as the B**** word then Third, they all were considered in his mind unworthy trashy, loud talking Ghetto-ish Sluts and Whores! Thanks to slave minded entrapment and Women unwilling to release the slave shackles after the freedom bells have been rung for so many years and the only thing that hinders Black on Black crimes and Women whom are free of being bucked by more then thirty Men, no-thanks to slavery!

The black Women is free seeming to forget the suffering of the ancestors. They don't speak the evils which occurred so the young Women are freely seducing and loitering and discrediting their bodies at alarming numbers with free will, just giving her precious body to any one rolling the dice! Repeating history is Men and Women who forgot are refused to study the past or their history. With her on purpose of self-righteousness and respecting her Mind, Body, and Soul. She became a diamond and as pure plenty as gold worth, she was rare unique and a prize well worth bragging about and not wanting to share!

She promised herself to love only one man and she loved and Knew who God is, this is the type of Women a man should always protect putting his only sacred life on the line fighting for something so precious, so pure, and so rare as to search for an Adult Women whom is a Virgin with Pride and Love for the Holy spirit and knowing understanding the history of suffering and sacrifices endured by our Ancestors!

<u>Chapter V</u>

Is Love Lost? What Is The Cost?

With pure will to triumph knowledge of her very own dark related history. She feels the pane by visual effects very sensitive emotions, she feels the hurt, the pane, the suffering of depression, oppression she yields herself to remain pure in her own sight. With her very own self righteous, purpose she claims to be the way in which God has kept her, guided her from falling into the large expanding always engulfing hungry Human Fly Traps! Which snare the dumbfounded Women whom Know the ugly truths, yet they continue to seek refugee in the Clubs and the unrighteous so called thrill to drop her A**, like it's hot, always shaking and popping her rear end! Always looking to see how big her rear end is as to want more attention, blinded by true logical realities, the ghetto life pulls many Black girls off track! in which they never Grow or become Authentic Women until they find Gods true Purpose Of life!

Respect yourself, mind, body, and soul, in order to become a true honest Women or Diva! Honor yourself and your elders, along with self dignity, self-respect and morality! One know and love God and his purpose. Then align yourself to find your true purpose of life believing in God even with your eyes close you will remain on tract as long as you have light and goodness in your heart you will never be defeated lost or destroyed, even when your afraid never give up even at times! If you think God isn't listening just remember, life is also a test of faith and will! Also strength and remembering the word and your knowledge of the world! Strong Women can conquer her own mind, with loving one self or God appointing you assistance to complete you in which you can be awarded in the essence of a Husband a companion to help strengthen you!

When you truly need the spine or back-bone! Slipping so far behind or under to the likes of the enemy will be unthoughtful of when your both in love and share the faith of loving and Honoring God together in prayer in faith, belief along with true genuine, loyalty respect for the thanks of giving, providing, protecting his loyal servants. Men and Women of Gods Divine Words. In it for the worth of ones own efforts to imprint an positive full sheet of completed words formed on blank paper which started off and beginning with one word!

After trials and owning life the paper that was blank has filled the sheets with dripping Ink with more words of Gods truths then any blank sheet of paper can sustain or occupy for the Word of God is without Boundaries or restraints of depths or peaks, expanding beyond the imagination of thought, or the limits of confinement, his word travels beyond every so called last star which is infinity, traveling beyond all Galaxies at the end and every beginning is The Creator. The one and only Alpha Omega, The beginning and the End!

Women whom repeat an offense of dooming the mind, body, and soul, If you have a daughter she is subject to endure the same exact tyrant and mutant excusing herself her deeds by repeating and opening the same revolving doors of the Human Fly-Trap! Which eat you whole mind, body, and soul. Most victims don't know how deep in condemnation their in because no one expresses the urgency with understood Hip-Hop or words of expression with unique expression or painting a picture, covering all angles and details stopping the excuse before hand, even before it is thought of speak and told your next thought, is so that we have a clear visual insight of contraceptive valued and your own self righteous perception! Even while it may be tainted it, is your own belief of injustice, which hinders your every judgment or beliefs, blaming, the mother, if the most important, Women in your life is your mother, the first Women you will ever love!

The most special Women ever in your life of existence, have no pride in respect for you or herself. How does she expect a Son or Daughter to grow up a Man or Women learning to love the Opposite gender! If a whorish Women raise and train a daughter to grow up and be a Women, after you were a poor example. All she knows is what she witnesses as a Mother of no values! Descent Women in your own eyes do you truly know what the morale defining composition of respecting ones body, mind, soul, means to the utmost of honoring God first. Your lively hood expresses the company you keep, the dread that fill your heart and soul tainting your mind as crippled and handicapped with thought and aspiration.

Indirectly a whorish mother taught her very own daughter how to disrespect herself, her own pride and dignity, using her body as a human slop machine or a tool to an mechanic, along with tainted and ruining her very own body while destroying her soul inside, she slandered the gender of Women whom were righteous and honored. God along with the purpose and their own selves respecting mind, body, and soul. Living without care or concern. She dishonored herself and her inner existence, the more she proclaimed to be gaining financially as she scored and accumulated large amounts of dividends, money grew and she became much more depressed as her client list reached and extended beyond what she had imagine. When she was badgered by family members of good moralities, whom warned her how she would become a feast to Men and become abused, used while being exposed to all sorts of scumbags! Predators of all sorts diseased and the mentally disturbed, she was insulted, considering to fail never to succeed subdued to the wrath of failing while prostituting, managing oneself as in a wager, bidding to purchase an wanted item of merchandise!

Repeating the footsteps as to say the apple don't fall far away from the tree? Knowing the way she felt about her own mother, while observing and witnessing all the men her mother served and slaved to sexually. This young lady at such a very young age seen her very own mother whom performed sexual favors directly in front of her own daughter, as her daughter had seen nearly every date her mother negotiated along with sometimes seeing their bare necked bodies, sexual activities which occurred while she looked on confused dismayed although hurting for love, every friend at school reminded her what the word. Whore meant while taunting her about her dear mother, embarrassed and ashamed remembering what she had seen thousands of time, she begin to hate dear mother and she begin transforming rebelling against all authority. Age 17teen she gave in becoming like everyone else losing her virginity!

Afterward an spiraling effect occurred in which she was

27

mishandled, misused having sex as an anti anxiety antidote, at age 21 she was so raveled she couldn't keep count how many men she slept with! Her mother voice echoed like a bad dream. Replaying itself repeatedly, quoting if you sleeping around having sexual relations if your getting laid you mightiest well be get paid! Using what you got in between your legs as a gold mine! Deranged becoming exactly like her mother, while producing large amounts of money. She became lost in a world careless conniving vandals with a future to be lonely and every suspected man who never knew your were a prostitute, became in your mind a number associated with who is next?

After finally giving him what he thinks may be long term. You can only vision a customer! Moving to the next client emotionless. A good girl gone down the wrong paths. As the Angelic beings know all the wrong permitted as you have drifted very far away, they attempt to make moves to get you thinking opposing the life putting, deep depression and reality in your life while counting hundreds of thousand shopping, spending buying expensive items damper you. Even more the life style taking it's toll, friends diminishes, while drugs emerges.

Habits and alcoholism becomes a very close knit escape. A very imaginary friends you taunt everyone whom said you will ruin your life and fail, you laughed in their faces taunting them by throwing a bundle of money in their faces! Nearly worth ten thousand dollars nearly, their entire income yearly which you earned. In just one night! In anger you stated this is what I earned tonight! Take it you scumbags! Who doubted she would be like her mother, amounting to nothing. Here it is nothing like her mother, she say's I am better then my mother! At an higher demand then she can ever accumulate as a Women of night! I am successful in my industries which a franchise not a crime, unless the girl has no class, therefore at high demand!

She is a upper class value at 3,000 every date per 2 hrs stay! All request are complied and serviced. Thoughts of the small young girl have changed, she chose to live without light or care! Diving into the darkness, she accepted her own demise of dooming oneself. Pleasant and pure one day, the next day she becomes raveled and whorish lost without insight or care!

Decomposition of gaining large sums of money while your face begins to vanish, becoming distorted in thought, the normal once innocent nearly girl is the tainted treacherous venomous snake bitten victim. Ready to cause more damage in the form of dominoes in effect. Destroying anyone in sight as choices and actions replay in reactions. When at a young age he or she has perceived all Women to be whores thanks mom.

Because one act or deed not considered by a parent the mother whom the child depends on to receive supervision, how can she teach a boy that Women are special! Avoiding his early years of perception of filth, seen visualized and computed as disgusting. Instead wrongfully teaching him how to hate Women because if a boy hates the first Women he loves! Depending on how she conducts herself, he will grow up a Man hating all Women always comparing them to his mother. Always searching for Women different then her even going outside of race searching to find a Women in his mind with-out fault. Forever damaged he became, one Women mistakes "effecting a world" almost like "Eve and the forbidden tree of knowledge."

Many Men and Women lost this divine spiritual reward, feeling of the up-most greatest reward. Women have become whores to Men and fornication, adultery crimes against the spirit turning something great into a profit or financial reward. They use what has been precious and instructed sacred for only just one Man, they share openly, transforming them into beast-like monsters. They lose the divinity in spirituality art of love-making with your life-time chosen mate! Women would identify and say they have felt this spiritual feeling with every-man, they have ever had sex with. Although they are lying and they are deceived, they only trust in their lust of desires to feed that lust with hate and profit obtained what you call satisfaction of the flesh! Some people may have had the feeling which was spiritual, divine in their purest state when you meet your soul-mate. Its not often, you find a soul-mate, if you do you will know. I promise you this!

If he/she happens to die, you can have sex relations with over a million others you will search this planet thoroughly. No-one will ever compare nor imitate this divine approach when you made love with your soul-mate the first. its one in 9 billion no-one can duplicate the sensation, the moods, the looks, the glare. the way two should release in an outer body experience simultaneously? Two bonded! Drifting into one state, out of time, sit stands still, and silence become tunnel vision, no-one can duplicate this feeling, God gift from the womb and the creation of Women, nothing compares to divine sexual relations of married blessed couples performing a spiritual inflicted sex exploited pleasure, which reaches the soul!

Two people are one in the moment which is explicit bonded, floating clouds grasping hands, and flowing electricity tingling the soul. I can grasp a promising, loving event to die for! In your purest form of love promising to be one forever. Once you break that oath even the love making is different, It becomes normal, regular like all the other sex, but soul-mates sits atop of the food chain! The best gift God have given man besides life, is someone to share this life with that is why a soul-mate is internal! It's that she is destined as yours even beyond life, even in death! She makes amends with God redeeming herself righteousness to become a child once again for the sake of holding on and not loosing your love. While she reinstate the word of God repenting memorizing all biblical terms. While the words save her and put her peacefully in a place pure to where even upon stumbling she can repent!

A chance to reunite with a new found discovery of beauty of the soul as the second reveals the purpose to save your soul! Working extremely hard choosing wisely the people who pretend keeping them very far way, seeking to misuse the blessings of God, Although the careless of God unless thunder echoes and wrath unleashes the bow down afraid, these are people unworthy of hidden valleys ordained powers greater than any thing seen or touched which heals cure and diminishes all evil spirits, from the heart of rejuvenated Men /Women who live understanding the rules whom knows the friction and recipe of defeating the realms of dark sexual evil spirits! The passage for men and Women Read the biblical terms and live by it.

Chapter VI
Soulmate's Bonded Together, Two People Enduring A True Love!

Women don't confuse the two, because those Men or Women whom have truly been in love with a soul-mate, they can identify with what has been mentioned, while the ones whom haven't will pretend because they are ashamed that they have slept with nearly 1 million Men or Women, they have never experienced that feeling yet! Ever heard of chasing the dragon the first time, first feeling of sensation every thing after is simulations. Truth being told lust is the reason that you think you have experienced love of a soul-mate, don't get the two confused. Why when you meet a man that is sent to you by God you will know? Study the order God send you blessing! Don't think you'll spend ions worshiping doing evil deeds that one moment you pray expect a blessing, it takes faith along with hard dedication, effort put forward executed with just deeds to receive just favor to obtain a blessing from above.

When you are in need, you may pray for these things. Look for the signs, the things you requested to appear in the form of this man, his traits are from God! His deeds are heavenly or righteous, his purposes are moral. God will not send a Women for a Women or a Man for a Man for sexual favors! That is sent by the world and the evil design in the form of lust and deceit. God sends a soul-mate his life is compatible to yours, you are like one you have met for a day or two but it seems if you have been around for many ions, knowing each-other. Feeling love that you shouldn't possess, because you haven't been together long enough! The brief time you have been together. You have become in-tuned with each other. See you have to study each-other, the people and ask God to open your heart to know what is divine.

If you are truly from God, with God he will open your eyes, if your not you pray to another god! He is your master of deception! He will use you and manipulate your every-thought to conceive that you are with un Godly ordained Men every time you sleep around but your are not with a God chosen man divine and ordain.

God sends you only one man to love spiritually! Physically only once, through sickness and health until death does ye part! Get it! "those are very important words" that imply with having and meeting and living with a soul-mate..." So please stop disrespecting yourselves" allowing Men to mislead and deceive you willingly because no-one becomes a victim unless they are forced and pressured against all their might and will voluntarily!

The divine plan to manipulate the Earth as our friends from heaven watch over us assisting us in speech and knowledge, grooming some of us for great rolls. That must play out in order for us to prosper and grow. We are like babies whom forgot how to smell, hear, touch, listen. The voice of God has always been around us his images has always been in the clouds. People have given so many testimonies! That we the people whom are not in-tuned, we disregard and disprove the knowledge that they offer or share it has not happened to us we disregard the stories out of the bible terms because a man told to build an ark has to appear to the masses insane, in our time if a mans says he has heard voices, we become hysterical calling him derogatory names and insist he go and see an shrink and get treated because he is not in touch with reality, truth is your not in touch, so you don't understand and you don't believe because of your programed, inside your mind a blockade exist, created to prevent you from knowing your hidden truths instead, influencing you to follow the lost into a world of trouble. So that they can miss-use and abuse you for there own lust and desires.

When they say you are being controlled, that is not literally. That is a fact! You have unseen spirits that attempt to invade you with out being permitted, Although you are created to deny them from the invasion of your vessel that you Captain and anchor alone, once your deeds become pure nothing un-clean can touch you. Does manure dwell on land smeared over your body? If it did you would have to be insane or you just be smelling like bowel all the time. It has a place where it belongs, separated from land pipelines are created so it can go in the ground. So that the smell can be smothered and prevented from surfacing on land!

Does a lion tribe and hyaenas commune with elk? They eat the elk! So how can good spirits dwell inside of evil things or vessels, that are un-clean they only can walk beside you and guide you in-order to enter they would have to put on a suite of Armour with a gas mask to prevent the foulness from being transferred, to enter your fitly vessels full of foreign germs. You would have to be purified, sanitized, washed and fully examined. With pure authentic holy-water which is the word and finding grace the word of God washes your soul and spirit water just cleanses the physical flesh. To prevent order and create respect and generosity for your neighbors around you and their smelling senses.

Clean spirits can enter that which is clean and that's the only way he shall. With words Jesus demanding evil spirits to come out and go into that heard of pigs, good spirits only want to open your mind to whats best for you and earth. Because you are part of the system and you are part of each other. What are dimension? Where do they come from? How do they get here? Why do so many people speculate about 3rd dimension to the 9th dimension is the second dimension death? While the first is life! Are these dimensions used after door-ways to channel in our deceased relatives? Is it our love that keeps them clinging on? Is it our memories that keep them here? When we stare at an old video recorded before their deaths or picture? The everlasting hope which brings to surface the thought of a pass moment, suspended in time replaying itself in our thought causing emotion's to re manifest itself. Is it our senses that create the dimensions that we say exist on total opposite plains, how do we know of a such place that exist?

If no-one has ever been there and back! Like the testimonies shared with you from people whom have witnessed the brink of death and came back to life? With an awesome dreadful or disbelieving vivid stories. Full of detail and insight of after-death experiences, how could any person speak of such existing places if they are not providing truth or proof, truth is not in guessing! Assumption is guessing, which is only a theory. " Theories based on facts and assumptions defines the hidden truth." Anything theorized is just a hidden undiscovered lie or truth. Facts brings light to theory with definition, proof giving theory of assumption a true meaning of details.

Thus as simple and possible in less complicating terms. With use of many words resulting with the same exact meaning or purpose of illustration to explain the true natural facts. You can be deceived or beguiled in the form of reverse psychology. Methods of word-play and word-positioning to process, theories and facts which can become distorted and misunderstood. Many words confuse and camouflage the truth which is buried with-in a sentence or story, like human corpses with-in the earth. Like a puzzle piece the more characters of existing letters complimenting words hidden messages lie undiscovered waiting to be deciphered. "facts or based on truth, details of truth are based on experiences."

The number 9 is the last number counted in equation, mathematically numbers are the reason the Universe is what it is mathematician wise. I normally ask myself if your taught to have belief and faith in religion why is it that mathematics are spoken of in regards of the Universe evolving, dealing with Orion's belt and distances to other Galaxies and Planets! With birthrates Social Security numbers, telephone numbers, binary codes and computers, time, television, adding subtracting giving or taking. The number nine is considered of great magnitude and the only number that revolves and repeats itself and order. Scientist have always argued the importance of mathematics' Discussing Einsteins theories and the importance of his solution of energy times mass. I really liked math, it was some what complicating. Now I find It quite challenging to conquer a subject which once gave me trivial conflict. I felt in heart why do I need to know anything about math? When religion is words of spiritual interpretation of reading and writing! I love taking on complicated task learning how to master that task and defeat it subjects. Becoming opponents, drilling myself to allow me to compete against myself! Similar to boxing matches never retreating. "I'm relentless."

Indulging in useless topics is boring and stupendously, miraculously,dumbfounding. Especially passive mortal mental injured individuals with out moral justice undeniably interrupted distorted by useless thoughts and brain material in the same regards as garbage, brain matter that is mis-used, un-used the mind of your regular every-day big dummies, buffoon, idiots, mindless jerks! Without sight or direction the lost but not found, whom seeks to be co-founded in due time, they fall all apart because they are speedsters that love the life on the edge. Becoming worthless expendables crash dummies, waiting to be re-placed, annihilated when on top they over use tyranny they are the toughest and boldest, yet the weakest, most cowardly lions, more like soft mushy marsh mellowly, fruity tootie, cowgirls disguised as cowboys, pull down their skirts, they convert back into that nutshell they hide inside.

It takes many to confront one strong-man. That's how the weakest people in the world combat war's, the largest and most legendary sophisticating crucial army ever assembled. They come and approach you in fear. But with that one strong man, he stands firm all alone. Because true men stands firm all by their lonesome! While cowards run for help and reinforcements, they truly hide behind their wigs of deceit! Their small miniature mini-skirts hiding their true vulgar identities. Strong in-front of the less mobile or less able to travel, anointing themselves falsely to be the all weakest in mind, true facts! When a man subjugate people because their inferiority, that man is just the weakest link! He cannot stand strong unless, he has assistance to crutch him up like a hobbling amputated one-legged man with-out stability or durability.

The moral of this! Is that most men even countries find belief in the wrong deities, causing the death even the lost of their souls even when they target other human beings that are unaware their punishments are that much more excruciating they only believe in things because they can perform magical tricks! It was written in the end time many false prophets shall rise! Performing great miracles in the land proclaiming themselves anointed as false gods, only deceptively misleading themselves into slaughter subjected to pay internally cursed by god for injustices against world-kind! Those whom are sacred mocking Gods name in blasphemy, compared to spitting in ones face in the most disrespectful manner of all. Which brings forth un-imanginable sin retribution. Which one can't tolerate for God is the true Judge and Jury.

So keep your noses clean a void temptation as much as possible! Try your best to stay righteous. It is easy to be evil. Although one must be disciplined and eager to do what is wright! Trouble is every-where, you travel most places you go, most people are not good people, so you have to go out your divine way to avoid hurting some-one or to keep yourself safe. It is so easy to hurt any one! A weapon of destruction can be accidentally pushed by an innocent child with-out intent to do harm! What it was design and created for is to destruct, see even children can do things to hurt people! That isn't the righteous way, when they are at the ripe perceptive age to know wright from wrong, they are accountable for there deeds so in the wrong or wright hands any-one can stir up trouble based on the situation and circumstances!

Change is necessary, change is important, change is suitable, also very detrimental. Nothing stays the same in-order to evolve, changing oneself, you must change your deeds, when you keep doing the same things, that caused you a world of trouble you become inflicted by your current deeds bound by karma. Committing the same exact thing that caused you much grief in your life. "Keep you stuck in that same stage of thought." Although when you change, you make things around you move out your way. With great results knocking down walls, shattering the dreams of the opposes, who pound their chest for results, that are negative and obscene. The so-called haters of the world. If you keep doing the same things you end up with the same results.

Pay attention to today's time which we are in a nucleus stage of prohibition! Our lives are changing right before us, what if in seconds I could tap into Gods hidden purpose for me and utilize it just for good. To dwarf all evil, rendering all perpetrators powerless. That they can't even pass gas unless instructed. The deception and cruel, unusual purposes of trying to manipulate masses becomes failure, it is always vital how they shall never be successful. Future times beware be prepared a time comes when cults begin to emerge using ancient tricks, defiling with sacrificial ancient Egyptian rituals, animals are forbidden sacred crimes, punished executed by God almighty for these heinous crimes are wrong it off-sets the order of nature. Indians believe that it is forsaken to just kill animals other than provided for one-self and family sustenance! In times of destitute. Trivia moments. Times have arrived when many regular next-door individuals are practicing black magic! Joining cults practicing witch boards.

The solar plain and Galactic changes the earth position shifting, and God is restoring everything back to normal, gate keepers are punishing the violators that commit the most crucial crimes against flesh in this domain. They face the most high wrath for whatever they done in dark hidden, trying to be covert with evil intent against flesh, they are subject for the worse kinds of retribution. God reacts in seconds, when it comes down to law and human flesh being violated without consent! You can call amongst family only flesh in blood. Through marriage you can commune with outsiders are forbidden to come against you, without permission no one is accepted in your home -- if they did not buy the property, they are not the owner. The only person that can denounce such forbidden unwanted guest is the head of the house.

The flesh father are the flesh mothering true form and by the word of God. The high most supreme almighty creator of just and righteousness. God of light and destroyer of all evil things. That a small whimpering, weak cowardly, shook and devastated person which is unwelcome in your home have no wright to remain once ordered to flee. They must go disobeying the true order that punishment is fatal, the human has all authority over all that is unseen, except that which is just and God sent. Under the righteous action they are allowed to do whats wright, nothing unclean or unworthy is unable to touch you are cause you harm body spirit or soul! For they all belong to the righteous true creator of justice righteousness and good moral. Protecting us under the umbrella, shield of joy happiness any thing that is good at heart in it's existence. No women man or child shall be subject to as a possession which is powerless against you, the power of your word when used against evil, intended intentions purposes are people whom are at the top of the chain.

Sending bad intentions directed toward your God almighty the true God of concern and care and goodness cut the

37

bud, nip it from the root from the beginnings of it's troubles. Render the enemy helpless. Don't allow nothing that is asked prayed upon spoken in this session to be changed! The heart word has been through much sorrow with grace and forgiveness with great wrath. Strike my enemy down show him your true powers! That are great show, him like David stoned Goliath, how Moses cursed the Pharaoh. How the floods lifted Noah and how in Sodom and Gomar crimes were offensive because they did file corrupted things! Show them your might, your wrath and power. Prevents them from returning, when they flee, for them let them be cursed, if they return after you have done your will!

Performed your miracles against a enemy that is mine and he is also against you! Which any-one against you is against me, may loyalty remain in the true people. Who have faith in you and those who seek redemption allow the doors that they, open knocking down barricades that stand in-front of them, that attempts to trap them let those deceitful doors that misleads one from the path of righteousness, be destroyed allow man know that the war is to combat the true forces of evil ones! Sent to oppress you in mind and body! Destroy their purpose, take that power away from them! With knowledge of knowing yourself and your origins, your creator and your purposes of existence! Ask yourself what is your purpose here on earth? Do you know the true answer? What does your body do when your infected with a cold? It's anatomy fight's off anything foreign, your white (tee- cells) defends your body. Now ask yourself what is your purpose here on Earth? Do you get the subliminal message? That you are keeper's of this planet in human forms.

When you plant seeds and crops they grow and develop into vegetation needed for nourishment in returns it provides sustenance to you in the art form of love and care! Yielding forth the warmth derived from giving in it's purest form. It is the order of life that respects life and life returns the gift back through sustaining life. When we have no respect for the earth she get's angry! They call Earth mother because the bible mentions description of the earth with words such as" she" or" with-in her" and it is understood that when something yield's forth something it brings forth life like a women giving birth to an child. "She

38

gives back to world-kind!" Oh! But when she is angry and mad at the world, she get's so mad, she tramples with-in this planet like a mad wind of violence or thunder and lightning becoming the elements of forces, which are necked to the normal human eye! Causing havoc and storms, earth-quakes and natural disaster can be documented, the earth repaying world-kind retributions for their unkind deeds of disrespect of her and the life she has brought forth! She has a heart-beat a energy in the core of earth that is compared to a Sun that emulates heat. Which can also bring forth destruction when her natural order has been interrupted and it has to realign the order of things, to get back into it's proper positions.

People suffer tragedy when she allows herself to blow off some steam. Like a volcano, after bottling up so much anger inside feeding off the emotions of the world! Poisons and toxins here on our earth that are released in the atmosphere, that effects her shield that protects us from foreign objects! Certain type of foreigners that are not agreeable with her, they only seek to do her harm. She had protected herself and world-kind with so many elements, that help keep us grounded so that we are not like hay-wired buffoons with out control. She has kept us with gravity protected against entering the Universe. Because it's told to human-kind that we can't breath in the realms of the stars and planet's that the cosmic dust of meteorites and asteroids would destroy us surely. At-least that's what they tell us, we have been told so many lies. There are so many truths, that are not meant to be discovered, so many hidden truths that are prevented from being discovered! And so many lies that hide the hidden truth's.

The secrets that no-one wants you to know especially the people who have attained those truths, they hide them from the true source of people who are natural born from the truth. So deceit was their major weapon. Awakening in the mind, releases the chains of bondage eradicating, the lies unraveling the people whom are chosen and anointed! To perform their true natural created talents that come from earth and above. The most high supreme creators of the spirit that is with-in our human flesh! Some people can remember when they were just coming in a big ball or streak of light, traveling through a tube and landing in-side the womb! Anointed with and taking that first breath of life! The blessing of life! So do you truly think that which is born is born cursed in sin? Is a child innocent when it is born? Knowing good are evil? A baby knows only to eat grow, observe, he learns everything through the things he/she watches, read, hear, some words are orchestrated re-arranged used purposely deceitful wrong. Teaching that child to be mislead, confused always searching for the correct directions. We continuously say that we are born in sin to our children! So they begin to always think they are some cursed child seeking to be forgiven. When they were innocent as babies, taught to believe that they are sinners and that sinning is their true nature! They grow up always mislead battling conflicting thoughts of who am i? Am i evil? Then they convict themselves taking paths which others had become confused and conflicted had took!

In this designed game of deception, that some tyrant has been manipulated, people have been tripped up along the way, we look watch learn and listen some of us follow people who we grow up idolizing the gangsters. We see on television or in the streets! They become role models in this deception. We have become the poor righteous leaders, in the sixties kids followed the path of the civil rights movement! Which now the rights are being Jeopardized! We walked miles together in rain! Snow storms with-out any worry about how we were going to get their. We got their! We didn't worry about where we were going to sleep! Because some one would provide you with comfort. The care was genuine! We had to look out for each-other! The newer generation of kids they don't anticipate the want to learn! As if they are under some sort of conditioned trans, they will read anything negative but they rebel to know things that consist of life and world. The earth's true essence to know who are their people? What we been through and what we have endured? How far do we date back in history? If more kids got involved begin digging up our history, the awakening shall manifest, we will be restored as righteous owners of our true essence.

If we had a massive attack of kids running to libraries and searching for truths. These so called black scholars understand, knowing of the politics that form tyranny and political progressive oppression and apprehension! When kids search to find out how deep their black heritage goes? Dating back to the stars! If knowing the truth their confidence will soar through the roof after finding the truth! They will wake up believing, that they are great, not because a black man was selected, let in to pretend he is Captain of the ship! He has the same amount of say-so that you have! "Understand." Why do we wait for white people to approve things? When they say it's OK or it's true we look to them for assurance and belief why? We know that they bury themselves in knowing everything they can find, be ashamed that they know more about your heritage than you know about yourself! They have always kept top-secret files, kept away in vaults that were put there and reserved or even some of the most vital important information was destroyed. We would never know we were trapped. The few of us caught up in a web of lies, searching for the wrong subliminal messages in each-other in the world. See the subliminal messages are when a person goes out-side, he looks around he see's a all black pole with a white sign that reads no driving or parking.

It's designed for you too see the white sign because blackness illuminates all things anything next to black it sticks out like a sore thumb. In the world-kind dictionary it is defined as not wright opposite of white, that is one subliminal message that conflicts kids that learned the truth! When they are taught they are black, they begin to identify them self. The same way the dictionary implicates or defines them not all kids fall for it. Until their eyes are opened, they start to realize that some people do look at them, like that, then they begin to wonder why. Sometimes these young black children ask there parents why some people don't like black people? We as adults some-time, some us haven't dug deep enough in history to ask why? We always wanted equality, so when we answered our black children we didn't truly know the exact entire whole truth. We always said; Oh they are just mean, bad people they don't like nobody! Or we gave some rhetorical answer; like baby it's because of our skin, is it any one that ever went deep into why? What did we ever do to become so disliked?

What did we ever do to become so displaced? Did we turn

41

on each-other and trade the less weaker, Up in coming stronger tribes for support of guns to get help in order to defeat nemesis tribes? That's part of it but, it goes much deeper than that one! That part reminds us that we have had war back in Africa! We have had fools who turned on others just for the greed are reward of gifts. Those niggers walk amongst us today, believe it when I tell you they sit next to you! Stand next to you! Talking to you and lying while doing it. Discussing how committed they are to their people! They are compared to the same ones, who traded their own peoples for weapons! The Judas mentioned in the bible who hung his-self, after realizing he made the greatest mistake of his life! See when you talk like this. People get scared ask yourself why? Ask yourself why do certain people get angry? Do they call you a radical that can excite a riot? Are they willing to allow you to exercise your willingness to express your wrights of freedom of speech?

When you talk about topics of race, people who care about their position in politics and the money have to be discreet. But those young men in the streets who talk about how they don't have nothing to lose, they can do things of great importance if they begin to find out who they are! Those whom are rightful in heart and mind, they will find the correct doors. The ones whom are seeking knowledge and they are tired of blood-shed of our people, a change must occur with them. They are the ones whom have to find their true nature and who they are in life not in death! Who your people come from and what they have accomplished. We allow this word subliminal distortion to dampen our thought! The first thing we trained ourselves to do is look for discrepancies in other people defaults. Something that is not normal are natural in their genetic make-up, pay attention to your judgment of characters while you venture outside. Watch how fast you look at peoples defects stereo typing people because of simple in-human reasons. Race and gender is always a every day topic of your life even sex. See those thoughts are the ones, We must learn to control tame not letting them control us. Look at a car, it's just a car although if you turn the lights on in the day time it sticks out like a sore thumb! Something is not normal! It now becomes a car that lights are on.

Look at your car when you drive at night! People will pass you by, blinking at you letting you know that your lights are off! You will turn them on the subliminal messages are people see thing's that are highlighted and it trains our thoughts to pay attention to the ordinary things that are perceptions of our minds. Which allow us to see things that are not truly what they seem. Even sounds are effective in playing tricks on us. That's why we listen and learn, how to be distinctive with thought our thought trains our physical body. We always find that we have a nature in us that must be contained. It is few of us who think we are to strong to become disciplined and follow order, live let live. Respect when you break those codes, you break yourself and that's when you find in yourself something that will destroy you! When you began to set standers of a unclean ungodly life, you got to know that some people are not ready for what God offer! That's why they don't understand simple terminology, God has worked in mysterious ways since the beginning, to find out the one's that must be annihilated they have no true hope or true direction! They only want power that's why they must be deleted! They only want victims. God fights wars along side Angels and people fight wars of flesh! We are in the middle of earthly affairs and heavenly affairs, that go way further than we can ever imagine! When we hear one thing and we hear other voices.

We get confused because confusion is the way to keep people in tuned to their true purpose. People get mind and thought raveled, mixed emotions. They become interlock with worldly devises and possessions. That's why they get confused when you not that pure, in heart you remain simple in heart! That is the only way when you deal with good people. They don't seek to hurt you are defiled you or disrespect you. They come to you peacefully but the ones who come to you with aggression and seeking to demise your end! Do you think it is formidable to turn the cheek, while you watch your family get mobbed and slaughtered in-front of your face! No-man will watch that, they will pick up arms and protect themselves! Against gangs, against any-one that seeks to inflict pain against them and their families. God fight heavenly wars Micheal is the Angel of what? Gabriel the Arch- Angels are what they are known to be! They fight wars against evil here on earth. We have been surrounded with fallen Angels! They have been described in this terminology to remain mysterious? They are warring to protect the one of the most important natural resources here, you must find your answer to this! Because now you are wondering what is resources? Search deep in your heart and find your answer's! They are every where all around you.

Books, internet, the bibles, holy tablets, the Koran.... Keep a open mind and read and if you have faith in God! You will learn all the truths you need. Pray for guidance to allow you clear thought and ability to perceive the true just moral values of importance, which allow you to over stand the important facts that are hidden in parables! In order to confuse the simple minded and corrupted disagreeable seeds of mankind.... Pray to the Almighty, The Alpha and Omega. The true creator of the beginning end. Whom gives the gift of life to all things, that exist in his image, in the name that is known to few. Respected by all that is unseen and unheard in the spiritual world. Mankind seldom visits in a clear sub-countenance state of mind. The Elohim, the twenty four elders whom knowledge and supreme powers are manifested greater than any humankind could imagine. The truth in Yahweh brings forth the deity of purity which is deep in the souls of men! Waiting for the moment to prevail, bringing forth everlasting life! As a reward to benefit the righteous men whom are loyal in mind thought and heart! Illustrating the gift of love and life without war and hate peace reigns supreme! Alleviating death and depression sorrow and pity.

Know who God is, feel his purpose and understand his true gifts of repentance and grace to forgive us even when we go so far into the darkness! Without all the sin, that can be rejected with just a small amount of faith, God can give favor and forgiveness to allow you back on the correct path! He knows that we are deceived by our own thoughts, that becomes cloudy but briefly and just enough time allows us focus and to become stronger! Resisting the hidden agendas of self-destruction. When we almost seem to give up on ourselves God, does things moving objects in places to allow us to get back into a good morale righteous state of thought! Protecting us just when we need it to forbid those unseen forces from violating our human rights of prosperity. Goodness and light dwells in the hearts of men profound unknown to most. Waiting to be discovered found and unleashed upon the world to enlighten each man of his true gift of life! Loyalty and love within spreading the joy and happiness of freedom and liberation of the souls glowing inner lights. That may be dim but oh they can be sharpened to shine all so bright! Illuminated clearly that is if you compare Gods true light you can become blinded for the Supernatural beings!

God manifest in spirituality shine so bright that one can, become blinded that illustrates the Power of God. Whom spares us so much for his love is great, his strength is much greater. Listen to the roar and thunder in the clouds when storms appears, notice how lightning causes buildings and the ground to shake, thunderously under our feet where ever we stand. In mere seconds night turns into day all across the Earth, natural fear consumes the human flesh, over whelming the mystic powers that sends shock-waves, through-out, the four corners of the earth piercing the clouds in the heavens! Grown men grab hold of their wives and children together as families.... We shiver due to the unknown forces of God, whom shakes and rattles the Earths core in order to briefly restore the natural order of the world! Giving us just a tad bit of his almighty powers. What we see in seconds brightening the heavenly skies thunder roaring menacingly louder than anything that could be imagined.

Thus, "what we hear", "what we feel", "what we witness" time and time again during the mystic storms as we hide when lightening strikes the earth! Our hearts tremble, our souls shakes in it's roots in fear of the great magnitude of powerful energy rippling massively threw the heavens. Silence preoccupies this green blueish planet in this stand still moment, as men seek to know if it is a false alarm. For ever most fearfully awaiting for God spoken, the words he shall come like a thief in the knight! With out being announced, no-one knows when he shall bring forth his finale judgments upon this planet. For once we realize, the true power that God has, along with his great magnitude of mercy. Strong fierce Men even hide always in fear, not knowing when judgment day shall arrive! The living shall be judged. According to his or her deeds conducted during the human trials

45

on Earth.

Notice how frightening short periods of outburst lingers during the thunderous sounds and storms, along with bright flashing lightning engulfing and shaking this earth to it's core. Every Man Women and Child encounters a biblical catastrophic moment if they have studied "The basic instructions before leaving earth " B.I.B.L.E.

The thought and memory of Noah and the doom and destruction of "Sodom and Gomar"! We haven't seen a place become obsolete due to Armageddon! God appointed disaster, we haven't endured a flooding that nearly wiped all of mankind population off the face of Gods green earth. We say that God voice is unheard because we lack the sight of understanding thought and senses. Moses or Mary mother of Yashua's. Noah guided hand and insight to build and obtain each beast and fowl insects in couples of two, Enoch, Ezekiel, Jobs encounter a test of unyielding loyal faith. Sampson strength, Davids courage, John the baptist, gifts anointed... Mary Magellan the repentance and forgiveness, KING Solomon knowledge of Proverbs, Psalms. The anointed star seeds, seers of God gifted prophets. Joshua bravery which launch the new establishing Kingdoms. Each persons importance set forth the waive of action one can't exist with out the other. This is what inscribes that my purpose is with quality and true meaning soon enough to be considered highly importance! These days and times we don't listen so we don't hear? Or we become confused with the new technology, we are so afraid that doomsday is so near! In our day and time. We are digging under ground climbing into the heavens in-order to run and hide from all committed sin

Believe when we hear the clouds shift and the thunder rattle the Earth, with it's magnification allure of lightening of nuclear booming sound, imminent and apocalypse, we run hide afraid to meet our demise. While standing accountable for all the wrong we inflicted upon the world. Small minded sentimental, unjust perceptions, which those of us whom are financially stern or able to buy positions are places that considered Doom proof!

We are fools in our folly to think that carrying out sin and pure evil intent in order to trample and oppress the less fortunate.

Obtaining so called shelter to avoid chaos and mass hysteria with wealth thinking that the wealthy and filthy rich would be able to escape the wrath of Gods punishment! The Judgment upon the Earth does not exempt rich and wealthy, excludes you from reaping what you see as if you give God a couple of millions. As you could afford to buy yourself. An VIP ticket or get out of jail free card! Forgetting that in Gods domain, money is less than the tree roots that you cut down to bring it to exist!" Man makes money" "God made Man!" So how can you bribe your way out of your vital troubles?

Mankind is so afraid fearing end time. Those of us who ruled with an Iron fist. We know that tick tock, time is near, misery loves company! Rather than choosing to do what is wright. The pure halfhearted Evil spirited people prefer to use all methods, possible to inflict Sin upon the Earth deceptively thought out to cause the few that are forgiven, finding the grace needed in order to reach an attainable peaceful place of joy, everlasting life of happiness without sorrow or hate and crime, lust, nor sin period.

Misery prevents one from finding Grace! Busy preoccupied worried about not getting in, they try so hard to sabotage anyone whom they consider might make it!

Sad to say even your own loving family would try to do things to keep you behind, finding deceptive immoral reasons to cover up the truths that they refuse to face. Although the truth always sets you free. The truth always shine brighter than any old pale face white collard lie.

No matter how deep we dig or how high we climb, no matter how stealth the man made air craft, that we travel aboard, our chances are slim to none! If it's ordained by the true righteous powers of God, If he permits and instructs our demise, which is instructed via Gods commandments. It shall come to pass, less God finds mercy and some good within, he is all that merciful as God. Although he Judges and committee many sinners to condemnation! Due to their ruthless crimes, without any remorse before his presence or past events without any mercy or concern to do something to repent or restructure the old to become reborn! Committing one life becoming an Evangelist putting quality time, foot work in seeking redemption and seeking out to save souls. Reaching and teaching the coming and arrival of the Law and the word. The enforcers of the grand engineered word of design. The creation and Judgment during deletion of Humankind on this planet called Earth. This is the purest and truest reality of the Bible prophesy's words of formality of creation and doom!

Chapter VII
God's Way Or No Way,
Crime Doesn't Pay In The End

Gods gift to mankind is life, our faults caused humankind to become cursed with death. Redemption of one sins along with repentance allows us to be forgiven. The nature of this world is confusing, the mystery in the Heavens are Mysteriously mind boggling.. Many People attend colleges to increase their knowledge of intellect and understanding, most People become more dumbfounded than when they had initially Begin searching to Understand the cosmic wonders of the world and beyond searching for more, wanting for more, needing more, although this big lie is the big truth! Believe it or not the world is captured in this World web of lies. Unraveled and in an trans like state people become tuned in to their phone, computers, televisions and they never come out of this coma state of mind!

This human made Web have captured many, while so many people are unaware that any such thing considered man made items becomes worshiped if it becomes more importance than God! You give more time to Idols / Items / Devices / Material / Man-made It then is in a way of covert trickery and deception, lack of reading Biblical and learning how to see entrapment. Becoming enlighten! It's better than the Web or Internet seeing and knowing who's who? When your soul counts on being delivered or swindle! It is important to see those whom are preparing traps for the sake of the demonic beliefs! Real; Oh yeah; its real as touch hearing and seeing!

The Bible protects you and it also prepares you to humble yourself. Evil spirits feed off rogue commotion, any place where things have gotten out of control. The evil spirits are working playing chest with every human involved time to them are as if it stands still. They wait for rage and excitement in humans to lose control to push you over the edge as to where you are unaware and respond I lost it! Meaning control and of coarse you do lose control although it's not all you, just as Angels pave your way doing good for you and guarding your aura, you can also phase

Angels out by living in darkness surrounding your life with evil.

Your deeds is the evil! The evil spirits consume you and keep you angry. The look is always in your eyes mistaken as tough it is actually evil trying too overtake you! You are always in control. Remember when you say I lost control you came back to reality to over stand that something attempted to overtake you! Although your soul and common knowledge and Aura awoke in an spiritual of self defense! Like a radar sensor detecting a close violation of ending its existence! It activates and the Guardian Angel who knew you at your purest state arrives and send all invaders running in a state which you are unaware! Good and Evil is combating in a very physical spiritual war to save your precious soul in which you take for granted by not reading how hard and how much God does for all mankind behind the scenes. Diseases, disabilities of mind body is something creating by the evil to weaken the minds. To weaken the souls of mankind in order to control and consume them in the end, so understand that knowledge the wrong way! Is just a diversion wasting time to keep you lost and studying the wrong way! Wondering the wrong way, thinking the wrong way, driving the wrong way, going the wrong way!

For example Human kind becomes to smart for their own good. Why is wisdom pronounced wise-dumb? Does this explains when a Human obtains so much intellectual inclination he becomes dismissive with the usage of common knowledge lost touch of the minor things, which are the most important factors of the world. He searches for Grander larger than life scientific explanations of things. Which he has been lead into conflict of theory and perception...The mystery of Heaven is meant to be unexplored, because we have not yet learned to have or live in peace and harmony, so how can we live with and beside something or someone that is not from this Earth! Without prejudice in our hearts? Maybe that is why Humans continues to search for Alien life within the Universe!

Although the Alien life refuses to push redial and return the phone call! Maybe they sit observing our every move, they are very familiar with our true human nature! Have they decided that it is detrimental that they continue to remain covert and in secret selecting very few whom they have chosen to communicate with and deliver their messages? An attempt to inform those whom attempt to search or find their secretive location and the mystery of their high caliber technology! "Quoting!" We come in peace! Don't you know they seen how and what peace begot the Indians! They have discovered that our Agendas of mass destruction is inevitable! A self-destruction exist to our own demise and thus as they remain in solitude, We continue to exist in division and conflict.

Evident or not we have been in contact with out even considering that God, have appointed many Men with a Gift, in which he attempted to create peace, through the words of average considered men. Who worked and was instructed by the spirit of God! History of Human existence is all the proof of the world Gods holy Imprint every where as you see the good that has manifested throughout the years, men did not discover fire because he was smart, he was guided to survive by the Holy spirit. Fire was created strength it prevented them from becoming extinct while they were prey. We have always been cultivated guided by many men who were good and evil. Every now again every few decades. We gained something of great importance, Fire, The wheel, Arrows, Spears, Building Communities, Cars, Flight, Plains, Boats, Guns, Books,Valuables to trade, Gold, Money. Computers Cell-Phones, Televisions, Entertainment which dates back to cave days!

The Messengers of God have lived with us and amongst us in an state unseen invisible to the human eye, the forces that are unseen but very present within many Humans. Shaping and molding the Worlds views and guiding Gods people whom learn to live through the most difficult instructions that have been written and studied! The Bible is our food, sustenance and instruction how to endure, live and persevere in life. The test of struggle that proves the loyalty and quality within a Humans heart. The Bibles mystery, the parables, the knowledge which the non-committed and loyalty of unrighteous people cannot understand the messages, because their views are tainted and from this world. They are unaware that the same invisible force called evil is also at work and every corner, where we congregate the evil is traveling within each man, child, women. Whom are living ghetto tough, you think it is you just being hard all the while an evil spirit trained in death.

The after death for so long watching preying on humans perfecting their abilities as how temptations occur as thoughts of something you know is wrong! Then you say nope I'll go home! You didn't know it, but the Angelic good Spirit attempted to save your soul, planting a thought to give you the choice and vision to detour from going the wrong way! Although we hear, we are just not attentive and alert like they were in the days of Noah! One step at a time which is hard work if you live day to day getting older and steady indulging in wrong, getting darker and darker until evil has fully possessed and took control! That's when the big Baddy Bang happens (Although Angels Jobs are very hard you see!) something strange and weird occurs like a slight whisper in your ear, is just an thought are assumption to do something that is down out wrong and senseless you get caught in some commotion things go all bad. The evil take control grabbing you as hostage while you are helpless now you can see an plot brewing. The evil Pilots someone else darker in spirit then yourselves, then out of nowhere you are caught in an situation you considered a set-up, your are helpless and now you need someone, anyone. There is not one single human around although, The Angelic Beings knew if you chose wrong, it wouldn't be a thing they could do unless God intervened. Sparring you a second chance with mercy.

God have mercy for those whom deal with mercy! He knows those whom have studied to know him! In this life and death moment, no homies around, no weapon, just you and fate and a God given choice to decide and choose what side is best for you to change your life by listening to the good in you. Which guides you or condemning yourselves by obeying the deceit within that is evil spirits plotting to overtake you with manipulation as perpetration in tough and the Ghetto way. Let no-one step on your shoes entrapment, The evil spirits is setting you up in a unforeseen world playing chess in your world, manipulating things around you. Then all a sudden you in prison for Life. Which is so bad because you can repent. Although with killing someone, It will forever be with you as you repent and change you will have pane within! Although remaining a young immature fool the biggest trap is how the evil spirits work conniving using trickery and all sorts of fools play, you are a victim of Murder, the biggest set-up permitted.

No one could save you the more evil you became, the further away from God you distanced yourselves! Then you where unheard because God lost the sense of who you were! Your beacon became compromised with darkness unlike when you were born as a new life and it shined bright like a Star Illuminating and glowing and the Angels Guarded and Protected You! The World Caught your attention you chose it oppose to ever knowing God! You never had time despite all the times God approach you in spirit, using people to say; hey son read the Bible even in a brief jail sentence he approach you through someone again, asking you to read the bible, every attempt so many times you declined the message, without truth the darkness was growing darker until your were unseen. When death knocked you called upon God! He heard but he couldn't answer. Because you didn't choose correctly or listen when he reached toward to help! You pulled away during the wrath as death pulled he couldn't pull you out as much as he wanted. He listened time and time again how the men screech and cry screaming. God help me please as they fade away from the light and breath is constricted, twisted like his soul is in the beginning stages of death! It pulls the fear of life being taken away in your purest state.

It seems as a dream although your countenance and soul can feel the wretched scorned souls by the Billions upon Billions hating you wanting to tear into you for the fact of being a living Soul! You scream for God to save you, if you slip downward, the Evil that is outside your physical flesh, surrounding your aura with darkness so that your soul is consumed body as well as soul and mind! Prayer is good because if your losing your family, prayers are heard and just maybe God will send Angels to pull them out. Although during this you are caught or spared by your own deeds, if you knew God or not is the most important factor! This evil the is unexplainable to the living and sinning. Although if you are free spared you may become a new man wanting to share and warn the entire World! That hell is real place, make amends repent pray.

Do what ever it takes, put work in save the fools who think death is a video game! Living day to day saying oh well I'll change tomorrow! People who are here with a second chance are working hard, they can become plague with evil spirits sense they are walking or have been to both Worlds. Invasions of the worse plague them if they are not doing what they need by God to reach and Teach the people when they begin to do Gods work. The Angels remove all tormented Spirits! Example Jobe in the bible was infected by evil spirits, they are sicknesses, diseases, and they continually think of twisted things that are mindless and full of filth, they want your mind, then, body in death you know whats next, just think of battling to think good and your a man and they attempt to implant thoughts to make you convert into an women, this is how evil works! This isn't a game they have been doing this for many years and they have gotten so good they have tortured men into submitting and for just a slight recess.

These men commit the worse Sin known to mankind, they have sold their souls and become workers in a network moving the physical objects which the Evil spirits uses them in order to get the jobs done. Much faster in the Physical world when they say the evil is running out of time, desperation implies improvising which this coming out the closet exposing themselves with the likes of using an Cult as an attempt to force many people to denounce Gods power and the belief as if they can Control their worshipers or slaves. They can perform magic and trickery to Ignite a New World Order, The plan is to over take the power and then The World! Cesar says strength is in numbers and if you put faith in God you can save yourselves, because you forget and think of The World and people chose by the World forgetting in death, the Set-up!

That's why this is so big and the chess moves are not just simple players, these players are actually looking for a good fight they have so many people tricked they are playing Russian roulette with souls. While the sleepers think its just a simple Game of Pawns and tomorrow you wake up blessed by God, That my friends ain't the reality You must become Awake and know that two Worlds are at work. The knowledge of the Bible is the only truth that can save you remembering the Bibles truth the evil only lies and hide behind trying to act and pretend to know the bible along with utilizing are trying to change the evil swarm these people trying to get them to comply and become pawns. Amazingly some people sold out easily with simple worthless deals, in this end time half in between people who know and worship God. Tryingly although not whole they are not as tortured as most, although some give in and sell out.

This must be let out they have this order of people practicing Dark Magic, Going into stages of possession and being overwhelm tied down inside held hostage because they fail to know God, this ain't the worse because death and Revelations must occur and the World will become lawless and the clues are being released in Movies such as Purge. You have one night to kill releasing more demons when the sins are being committed! The lure to transform mankind into this lust of Zombies that are mindless and reckless that it may shoot and kill survival of whoever got more guns shelter and supplies and bullets, this is a intertwine human and evil spirit premeditated plot! Which is evil and nonliving cares less about life! Some humans have seen much more in places which are off limits to the World.

Although they have engineered a Plot attempting to foolishly condemn themselves thinking they are being impressive sacrificing human souls humans are tricking and enforcing people to transform into this new world order and it was secret now they want the world to know and they want the world to fear them and they are recruiting daily, people are selling out Physically and losing out their souls, the most important chess piece they are loosing with the most simple move of all not knowing how to listen to their hearts and souls! Following what is simple the broad in correct road. The horror of death is being sugar coated, hell is being made up to be a disco so many false lies are acting as if they have seen hell and if the are spirits from the dead that have risen stating and acting as if hell is beautiful! It's in our minds on earth. When you awoke your mind can see color smell, thinks, roses are pretty women are beautiful!

So if you can see all of Gods creation Hell is never in your mind if you can see good. Hell is after death and according to your deeds if you shall be cast down to the bottomless Pits! Earth is created by God, terminate all living creatures and observe the beauty within the earth. Quote Earth is not hell. Sin of deed and Evil have created a place which those who are all evil whom refuse to become good in heart, they must be imprison for ever to eradicate the evil on earth. They want earth to be their Evil domain. Although the evil In hell is too much for them to bear so they hide and run to evade being condemned when Judgment day becomes a reckoning and Gods commandments are spoken calling upon all his Armies so that not one single soul or spirit slips through this funnel of cleansing and destroying all life not just punishment just a beginning to that which is ending!

Sorting the good spirits from the bad and that which is evil gets locked away in its own domain, misery love company! While a new clean earth and heaven is restored! A captured slain soul of evil, another senseless foolish victim appointed to dwell until Judgment day! Planting a thought to detour you from taking the wrong path. The prevention and Angelic beings! Anything opposite is forces of the deep below shadow world of Darkness! Why was Jesus sent here? Did he not mention that his Kingdom is not of this Earth! Which explains that if we as Humans crucified Gods sent gift, a messenger who taught the people the way of the Heavens and how to gain entry despite the dedications and practices of preaching the knowledge performing miracles, the people did not believe that he was a (Son of God) How can we live amongst God? After all Mankind murdered his only begotten Son! The Bible speaks how Mankind had attempted to build an tower that could reach the Heavens, in their folly their tower was destroyed! It had been toppled, the human race was scattered and their language was confused as they begin to Babel, that word is prominent in today time defining a Mans vocabulary and words that are confusing and unexplainable! The search for more is what Humans fight and race for, who can achieve obtaining more nuclear explosive devises and advance technology.

The truth is the political views are deceptive we say we are peaceful when an foreign invader arrives, although we are actually attempting to deceive some one whom has been around much longer! What if they can predict the future? How is a lie considered truth? How is Mankind considered loyal when his exploitation and actions proves otherwise? How can he expect to receive, what can not be understood? When he himself is confused and attempts to blow himself up, would he then turn on those far away? Then attempt to use such a weapon or high end technology on those whom are visitors? Like a Father and Mother who teaches an child, When that child attempts to divert from the teachings and lies about the mischievous conduct, a Parent knows and predicts the results of outcome because the Parents were once a child so he understand the way a child thinks... The term and statement I have did things you are doing, so don't think you can deceive me with flattery, because I gave you a chance don't think that you were sly! I allowed you to prove your true identity of the heart condition and compassion to do what is right! Thus the words a Man is measured by his deeds and actions!

So why does a full grown Mature Man thinks that if Messengers of the Heavens descended upon the Earth! That he is cunning enough to pretend that he is peaceful intend to perform good deeds on Earth if permitted or allowed to receive advance technology that is fully capable of many wonders. We are tested observed studied. Just maybe it has been this way for centuries! Don't you think that is why God was very careful to choose a virgin to give birth to Jesus? And very very careful whom he had chosen to write the scriptures of the Bible! Even that much careful when the chariot of fire took up Enoch, Elijah and when the burning bush allowed Moses to understand what the Ten commandments of the world would be. Martin L. King he was also a messengers of God. All Twelve disciples were attempted to be murdered, Eleven of them were delivered into the hands of their oppressors for preaching the word of God. Martin L. King was also murdered for attempting to liberate and declare that all men were created equal Although the evil in many Men hearts disapproved that Black Men were equal counter-parts!

Considered inferior to the supposedly Superior White Human race of People. If Men are Killed performing the practice of peace on Earth. Are they not doing the work of the high almighty God? God has used paved the way for Mankind time and time again! Why does hate exist in Men hearts? Until their unruly demise is presented before them, they beg for Gods mercy, after inflicting a life time of misery upon massive of people whom seek to find Gods purpose of life! Why do Men commit acts of evil consider it an act of God? God works in mysterious ways although when a Man kills for fortune and Greed no true Purpose, that is not instructed from God. That man is not a Man of God. His heart has become tainted! The Bible mentions there is a time for everything! I think a time to kill is when you have Men like Hitler, that kills Millions of good God fearing People, attempting to rule and conquer the World with an Iron Fist of fury and death along with evil intention and Tyranny!

Now this explains why God would anoint his own Human Army of Men to be lead and risen to defeat any such Human possessed. With an overwhelming evil that devours his soul. Greed and power becomes his unreachable Goal, the root of his own Demise! What Kingdom has ever been left standing after challenging Gods Might and Will? I believe there is not one single Kingdom on Earth that have continued to exist after the wrath of God's fury. God may have found mercy and allowed the seed of sum to rebuild in different remote parts of the Earth, understand it was only Gods mercy which allowed men to regain their assumed Positions! Men of NASA attempting to obtain things which you have no true understanding of man, although God understand and have an broader understanding of all humans deeds and true nature. That which is given has been done with a greater purpose than any human shall understand why!

To think one deception is unnoticed is just folly to the creator and a recipe for self-destruction! All men shall be Governed by his own thoughts and deeds rather it is good purpose or unusual cruel intent.. No-one can know the truths of the Heavens and live amongst men! The things that Men think they know are only the things he is allowed to know! Understand why Babylon, Atlantis, the city of babel tower was destroyed! It was not yet time for Men to explore the Heavens, Like a child Mankind is immature, unworthy for such inclined Gifts, Like a child, mankind fights they have temper tantrum, like Kane.

Mankind is jealous of his own brothers deeds and seeks to destroy any man that gets closer to God, then he himself! Mankind seeks to explore the Heavens in peace, yet he has not found peace on Earth! Man crave for war!

Mankind shall you say we come in peace? Yielding an sword in the same motion? So how is it that Mankind thinks he is worthy enough to live amongst God? While he is ruled in the way of the Earth and the evil that exist within? What is your true desires? What is it you truly wish to Gain? God knows the answer, although you must find your truth to this question in your Heart! Sincerity is what God sees in all men whom attempts to hide their truest motives of deception.... It is the bible that describes many stories of many great men and visitors not from this earth, which in other words, if one does not belong to a place, he is Alien to an foreign land. God is the truth the creator from the heaven of the Spirit. "He is the Alpha and the Omega, The beginning and the End!"

"The Human hardwired Brain computer or Human Flesh?" Human concept and thought is very vital at the beginning stages of human life within the wound of the carrier advanced formation begins divine Spiritual intervention takes place. Brain waves and patterns creates the genetic codes of that child, the electric current that flows in the wound of the mother/carrier of the child can be very significant to the birth of an scholar or an scientist in the mold. The mothers every thought becomes one with the child all that she endures emotionally transfers all data entry from her to the wound where the child is housed like an assembly line 9 months of preparation to the 9 power and the greatest number and the last number which multiplies which produces an product of human creation in the art of pro-creation! Involving male and female.

There just might be an day when mankind creates human life in the same fashion how an Car production assembly line produces and builds vehicles. How ironic it would be if this became evident and possible sort to speak when machines are developed to replace human workers. The humans that are replaced by machines are terminated from their appointed positions thus if life is some how fabricated with the help of

59

technology, will we allow ourselves to terminate the women positions will she be considered expendable? With the emergence of cloned creation and Homo sexual appeal of male genders is it that much easy for an gay man in his own rights to forget the existence of women destroying his ultimate competitor? So that he becomes much more alluring and the hottest commodity on the market!

I can only imagine with certain events and newly passed Gay wrights and laws what may happen to lie ahead in the near future? Mankind is always at work thinking up newer advanced ways to consider themselves reaching newer pinnacles of apex agendas, the problem is the one time he makes one big mistakes and technology begins to backfire and extinction becomes inevitable. Curiosity always kills the cat! Especially if his curiosity leads him into a deadly situation beyond his knowledge and realms of agility. If the creation of human life can be duplicated with technology. I do believe more sexist gay laws will surface and the women net worth value shall decrease with the almighty politicians, scientific views happen to become more like religion. The purity of women, her smile and soft body with bumptious curves her flesh, her soft pink lips and smile.

How can preposterous technology replace the realness that women are? I have learned to appreciate and love women as a man! They appeal to me beautiful and loving. I have a burning sexual desires to lay next to a soft beautiful smooth skinned women with breast hips and curves consumed in a bundle of compassion, holding each other kissing the gift that is meant for opposite sexes male and females, while this Women is a gift from heaven as a wife sent from God. Which means she is more precious then gold and should be treated as such for her days and nights will be honored only to thee through sickness and bad health, until death does us part. This gift is from God. Not mans confused thought of male and male, just because he wants to play 8 ball in the corner pocket! Brush frisky beards like Pirates. Women were created for the accompany of Men due to his lonesomeness, Women happen to be the next best gift, God had given Men besides life and the breath of air.

The facts are what if Gay rights are permitted so far along

that creation of life is advanced and formidable, if the many Gay men obtain power. Will they attempt to turning the world inside out considering women useless terminating their only competition? Now the world in their eyes becomes one big Gay happy place to live for them, for now they intend to replace the real women and when a child is needed they will go to the labs and print one up. Will this one day become a part of history? A true reality when women are forbidden to give natural birth and she becomes an fugitive at large because she is female. A rare demand and nearly extinct if a man posses a women she is like rubies and gold. This is just what if! Just thought of fictional imagination but if you can think it, can it happen?

During the day of the Neanderthals women chose the strongest defender to protect them in a strategical stand point! With out any ability or skill-set of defense of oneself. Her swift thought and Brains seem to work for her fairly well, the fact that she was a very rare but high commodity which the cave men had killed for, the rights to claim the women as his own property. With out any (say so) she had to use brains over stealth, as these ape-like animals fought like savages for the wright to mate with the female which meant death to whom ever stood in the way.. Sometimes exceptions were made if a women was captured in clashes of other rival Cavemen. She became a Prisoner of War normally she was claimed or shared amongst the tribes members until she escaped or until death. Law being non-existent. Women were treated as slaves until those disgruntled emotions evolved due to intimacy which seem to be like music to the savage beast!

Satisfying his thirst with confusion and also relaxing him as the women became the object and target of his sexual exploits! Realizing that she had a deadly weapon just as deadly as the Neanderthals Spear! She begin to think hard and long in the same since and creation of fire, she had come up with one Of the brightest Ideas as the lights lit in her mind. Realized many facts which made her a deadly weapon while she had been a Prisoner of war 10 years went by as she had been passed down from Neanderthals after Neanderthals, she realized that she held the power and she would use it to gain her respect and righteous place in her newly found Prison. Which had now become her home. She noticed how the many mixed feelings her counterparts all were products of this deep passion for her. So she used it to cause inner conflict with males who testosterone levels begin to cause brief altercations for the say so of breeding wrights.

She knew that she would be able to capture any of the males of guard during his most vulnerable, weakest point which usually resulted after the ejaculation! One mind seems to be cloudy after the brief explosion of emotions, growing weak in the knees the male Neanderthals shivers and clutches the ground out of strength and wobbly barely able to stand, she notices the plan of attack and orchestrated a plot to counter her oppressing abusive sexual partner with an altercations that would put two giants against one another as she sat back and watch the annihilation which she had planned for her rude oppressor to fall while he was weak encouraging the younger male that she had favor with and control of his rise was now, his rule was destined. She had an influence which weighed heavy on the younger Neanderthals. He could taste his victory as the new Chief. He would have to kill the old Chief in order to claim all the spoils. He was unaware that the wild Women had diabolical plans of becoming the new Chief. The women behind the man. So of coarse Year One of the Neanderthals Rising from the caves. Women have been one tool of ingenuity and a bargaining tool. Once women learned her importance, she became controller and ruler of her destiny. Queen of her world!

Shaping and paving the way for the many women thinkers who marry men of valor. Women nowadays negotiate for money. During Neanderthals time it was for protection. The facts are most remnants of the past continue to be a product of the Future as certain qualities continue to linger especially with Jerry Springer, Cheaters, Maury and all the many Ghetto fights over he or she is mine, she belongs to me! Brawls that verify we have continued to live with Neanderthals' DNA being pivotal imprinted in our genetic strands our ancestors as they scientifically say are extinct. I think they are so scientifically wrong! I also wonder can they explain why the apples don't fall to far away from the tree? If the neanderthals are extinct? We are one in the same with many attributes of past cave dwellers.

The mind can be space, it can create or destroy, posses emptiness or fullness thought which manifest creation like a solar system stems of neutron and protons in this systematic design great things are achieved with much enlightenment, waves flowing fluently like electricity sparking like light bulbs of genius thoughts transfer data like Einstein, the spark determines if one is sophisticated with wisdom or understanding many things which creates confusion. An empty mind is a mind void of the gift of life space taken but wasted, not occupied because no one occupies this place which is empty. Home alone the foolish lingers and are controlled like an army of Ants very low waves of knowledge travels inward or outward. The world greatest teacher is the Bible, facts on how to live and how to die. How to build foundations and prosper, the best teacher is life and old age! Memory kept produces reviews, studies of data that is stored away to study the straight and narrow way. Mistakes and human errors perfects the virtuosity of all men valor and public personification of mere singular personalities. Become morally profound and performing just acts, forsaken the deeds of wicked unjust and unrighteous men, whom seek doom death and destruction of oneself and Human kind.

Attempting to tempt the hearts of men who succumb to one vital material or false idol, in which a man grows to treasure with sentimental value. The way is to care about how your efforts of hard work and good deeds obtained such items, don't consider any thing that you obtained more important in your heart than the gifts from God. Life, The Word, Truth, Loyalty, Love, Respect, Honor for creation and the Gifts you are rewarded and the Blessing begin to flood the gates. God opened to reward your duties of commitment. God grows proud when people of righteousness fight the worldly temptations and deception of idols and allure, seeing the entrapment before the plan begins, with Steadfast and strength of mind, body, soul defeating the test and learning how to correct mistakes not every one can see the darkness that lies within men souls!

People become so endured with being hopeless. Sleepwalking becomes a way which is considered normal or average. The saying bury one old way once you have found and discovered your new self. The vulgarisms must become absent or dormant within depleting the deep sin. It takes time, a leopard does not change it's spots over night, gaining advancement to channel emotions which remained locked and invisible. The unrighteous life one endured, while doors open with opportunity, the heavens above rain down on you shielding you from harm. Blessing you with the acceptance of a new life rewarded gift. Separating gloomy clouds of distraught feeling of worthlessness and displacement feelings of a rainbow bright joys and happiness invades your life taking complete control.

What is human life with absents of God? The teachings living by the world in the life of joy, happiness. Lies and deceit makes you feel hopeless, defeated, failure depression which you endure the word the truth the more you listen to lies and believe the word of God teaches you how to verify the truth and decipher the false prophets. Who have no faith in the word! They believe it's false beliefs and half truths. When you stumble get back up try again even if you make mistakes with your loyalty with God keep trying disregard the thoughts of suggestion of deceptiveness! Which attempts to plant seeds of thought in your mind, this is how you defeat it, keep remembering and study Gods truth that highlights the lies that begin to run out. They are no more of good value or hope, so you know they will search many ways to distract you.

Defend yourself while falsehoods attempt of playing God transpire! Don't anoint a lie that you never knew. Never believe the truth about what some one else says, if you hadn't seen it with your own eyes! The eyes aren't always all reliable. The Bible attempts to teach you how to use a gift of righteousness. That clears all the deception of darkest evils! Dooms seekers of the bottomless pits. Don't fall for the lies that you are not good enough with low self esteem! Proof of worth is with God no-one else determines if you are destined to destroy, God gives life to the deceased he can take life and create life! Forgive while you prove your loyalty. Never Give up on God no matter what the perception is? If a thug swagger means burning and fire, I'll be a square from Delaware.

I refuse to be Raps music personification protege as Hip-

Hop persona Ghetto hood failure entrap. When I am the hood approval from that world is only to advancement of profits gained! Or else being cool to be accepted if that is the lie told then deception is exposed. God warns and instructs his followers to beware of foolish men and steer far away from their way. Foolishness is the deeds rules of life of selling out afraid to accept God! Afraid to repent giving up completely. Hope is God and faith is a gift if you stand by faith and execution living by the word avoiding deceitful people they are no good for the sake of your life. Steer away from their lies, the way they are ruled, the life that they live as imposter's like the crab mentality, they seek to gain company of misery scratching and clawing pulling down any and every one who see to break free of the clutches of demise!

Women are utilized as designed weapons, to entrap men whom may lust or crave some sexual desire. Just like Men all Women are not all bad, some good Women have good virtuosity and refuse to allow themselves in physical concept to become such a degraded commodity of exploitation of one self, as a financial gain or vindicated profit of worth due to the elicits sales of one gender and body parts! Emotional desires are gifts awarded to the soul mate whom you anoint yourself forever till death! Anything else is deception and should be avoided less you hate your soul and you hate life and have no respect for the true Alpha and Omega!

Chapter VIII
Man vs. Machine

Traveling in the Myst of the darkness, the date was September 23, 2008 earlier that day I had cooked a pot of beef stew sense I was home. My wife had been at work, she was a janitor, most days I drove her to and from work In my 1998 Ford expedition, we possessed three cars 1995 Pontiac Bonneville and 1974 Buick Century which became my hobbies, I bought the Buick after seeing this raggedly crashed old vehicle sitting next to my Cadillac El-Derado as I was on my way to school through all the ugliness. I seen a car saying help me, I saw beyond the outside where it had been seriously damaged on the right side, in traffic I retrieved the drivers number and offered him$ 300 and bought my first project an old school fix it yourself classic vehicle, this was three years before my deadly face-off as "Man vs Automobile" year 2005 during this time I worked a poor man hustle net $2,500, my Job payed me $2,500 monthly and My child care Issued out $898.00 a month, I was Full Guardian of my children after my Children Mother's death in 2004, I also received

$1,900 not including the wife$ 2,600 a month. We were set we received altogether at least $900 worth food stamps.

My Children mother had been murdered by some fool name fat-rat from 52 Hoover Crips while sitting in the front seat of the car in California paralyzed in a wheel chair he was arrested released after she was murdered June 4, 2004. What hurt engraved deep into my heart and I became shallow seeking solitude engulfing in many bottles of Hennessy and beer to sooth my pane! Me and her had more than just puppy love we had bonded and became soul-mates which we became one unit I protected her feeling as if it was my soul purpose. When she died I felt it was my very own absents not being their to help her make decisive humane decision, we practiced and learned teaching molding one another. Securing the others safety, the care was express so we were that much more in love still I think of her everyday I pray God can protect her in her dimension and domain in the after-death! I was 17 she was 15 we met, we had three children.

We separated she decided she needed space after my multiple attempts to patch up our problems after returning home she declined with my extended hand saying she had some one else, she didn't want me any more I crumbled as hardcore thug, I had been abandoned by the only person I had ever told her I loved her and wold die for each-other, 1998 I served Ten and a half months in LA County jail moved to Chicago, 1999 I met a female! 2004 after my children mother's death, she became my future wife, the fine big booty women next door, we were highly attracted to each-other with out a doubt, she lived next door t o 6748 S. Perry to my mother. 2002 I took a two week leave of absent from work, I went back home after being home sick. It was the best thing I had done, I had missed my children mother and kids! I hadn't seen her nearly four years, which was the longest we were apart, the feeling was mutual, she looked at me when I pulled up in the rented car strange, she said Big Ray!

Almost to say as if she was astonished, she talked to me on the phone at my job In Chicago expressing how she needed recess, time off with our bad children, things were intense she was discussing how she needed 6months to fix her problems!

Working and saving her extra monies with her C.N.A. Job. She was certified. I promised in a month and I would be their to pick them up and fly back to Chicago. She agreed although, she assumed I was Joking! She forgot how I did things after she had been dealing with scavengers, after we separated. I sent her money when she asked, I never refused her, she was the mother of all my children. After nearly 85 hrs OT. I earned nearly 3,000 dollars that month along with my side job called hustle added an additional 2,500! I was ready. I purchased 3 one way tickets a rented car and some new clothing for myself.

My children mother didn't notice me. I had arrived, I was anxious desperate to see my Children Mother this picture I took it would be the very last time I would see her again our two wonderful weeks she would share with me I never knew that the 6 months she needed would result in her running the streets care less resulting to her being murdered while I took care of the children. I would have never allowed her to talk me into taking the kids period. She seemed like her section 8 was being terminated, only one knew the truth was her uncle Junebug. He wanted to put me up on somethings! Although his niece begged him to remain quiet. He notice I had financial funds to fix somethings, her pride was ultimately interfering. She didn't want me to know the Lowly secrets.

Her house was immaculately furnished I couldn't since any discrepancy. I was excited four years passed we barely talked I was usually sending her cash through Western union after being threaten for child support, she was just bluffing because I sent her cash nearly every pay check! I wanted to touch feel and hold he the old days. Thoughts of sexual lust played out in my mind, although the desire was strong my juices had swelled at mere sight after she had me drop of my youngest son at school, we unloaded my luggage inside her home, we sat in the car having catch up time. I talked to her in my soft voice, where we going to go? What hotel are we going to? Then I thought about my gal in Chicago, I said to my children mother, I got a Good Women at home waiting for me and I can't destroy something good going backwards! I see you ain't change you disrespect your baby father Pete when he came over, treating him like a nobody. I was able to relate and remember how I was treated like Pete things were all bad. Pete was the man you chose over me, I sat In the rain coming to save the women, In 1998 I tried rescuing her from the world abuse and herself after, I was released from prison.

My baby mom appearances changed, she looked like something had happen! I took control which she hid her problem, I had always protected her! I smoke her weed, I begin to have faster then normal heart beat, she cursed me out to never touch her dutch. I called It off too never touch her green, when she put me out! I never thought it could happen? While it was raining. I caught the bus outside her and Pete stood inside walked out our room in her panties. Pete was behind her, the kids waived by! My muscular built body I had ripped the frame of the bar door off the hinges, creating damages and a Entrance. While I was intoxicated, she threaten to call the Cops, If I had repeated the act. I refuse with rage. I had never seen a boy with my girl in my house! After 8 years we were together this was unordinary, all I could say was one day ill be some where and I'm gonna say remember the time you made me stand in the rain? You will remember every thought and feeling non emotion or may it be payback in your mind now! I left!

2002 Back to Cali she grabbed my blank inside my pants, we sat inside the rental, she said I want some so bad indicating sex. I teased her talking about places, we had sexual relation, that were the best. She painted the picture! We reminisce about the Roosevelt park, Grape street the days I got out of the County Jail! The day I paroled from Prison, she came home the day after I was released from C.M.C where Suge Knight was imprisoned. We had the moment where we had an hotel room the first prison sentence I had paroled from Folsom. I caught the plane home, the first time thanks to unk. I was anxious, she was pregnant in two months after I was out. Living in the Garage at Aunt Barbara. It was the love boat we got freaky many nights even while being pregnant with Marty-mar nay-nay was 8 months, she turn 9 months. I went back to prison for one year. 2002 I pulled out bundles of money to illustrate to her that I was altogether assuming she would be proud I was mature since moving to Chicago. She ask me to count the money. I gave it to her a expression that your are always my Queen my number 1 lady no matter who? Or what you do! Or who you with, you will be #1. It was a mutual feeling. We both matured even though she had a child by Pete.

I was well over that blow, she took $300 put it in her pockets! I said nothing, she was mesmerized. She stated you leave me and become a baller! She knew if I didn't complain, I had plenty of money! I replied I work that's all! I saved up, I was so happy to be home in L.A. although my children mother hadn't changed she left out partying all night. I was the visitor, she hid my keys, so I was stranded unable to visit the homies in the hood! She had me hostage! She swore I wasn't going any where. I slept on the floor with my kids. Her uncle June lived with her. We were super cool, I bought every body food. Big round 5'6" 398 June was happy to get the food I bought for everyone, pastrami burritos and pastrami chilli cheese fries. I had been dreaming for nearly two year to eat, My very two last weeks I would ever spend with or see my kids mother again!

It was special out of this world. We had both grown older. I was enjoying my entire week laughing at her how she was still snappy, she went off on her neighbor for staring to hard at me, I laughed saying man you crazy! While we unloaded more luggage, we went shopping for the kids I also shopped an brought my step kids some jackets. She didn't appreciate it so she made sure at target she got my kids as much as she could spend. I went at least over $500.00 with my credit card. I then went to the jewelry store she forced me to by her a $300.00 necklace I didn't refuse I spoiled her. I bout her anything she wanted! With her I knew she would die for me! I would do the same for her! There wasn't a price or limit on when some one love you opposes to someone setting you up to die gaining profit while your dead. We traveled L.A day and night, she was my designated driver of coarse. I kept bottles of Hennessy we partied joke had fun me and Pete shared a drank! She was in the process putting him out that day.

How ironic I moved on increase my life and living standers and she had dead weight. A new child by a dead beat dad, he needed her or else he was homeless! I was in his shoes though I always found ways to get food cars and money! I was a hustler who made something out of nothing! I been gone 4 years and Pete grew a ruff beard and a beer belly. She talked about him so bad it reminded me of days I was with her! It turn me off, I told Pete how can you take this abuse man? You see why I left? She heard the conversation, I was trying to install some human marbles in Pete, he seem busted or deleted while the children mother said Pete you getting the hell out! My real baby daddy coming back home! I question who? She says don't play! I laughed, I said you and Pete are a beautiful couple! He need somewhere to stay don't put him out! She said oh yes; he out! All I had witness, I knew I would move Into a nightmare! So I tried to save her and Pete, she was serious she put him out with the last word! My husband back, after Pete left out. I said ummm when you get married? She got close nose to nose she was very good with seducing me! she got close nose to nose. She said you not going back to Chicago!

I agreed almost thinking I wasn't going to return! I had no true reason to return so I was thinking the women I grew feelings for I had been with 3 years. I did have strong feelings. I felt something, while being with my children mother. I missed her and appreciated her how she was matured and older! Which I thought was strange, I expected fighting and arguing, she was just perfectly opposite. She never called me I called her! I guess she assumed I wasn't never returning back to Chicago. I almost didn't return. I had so much joy with my baby mother, allowing her to take control buying what ever she wanted! She wasn't use to being spoiled picking expensive item counting my money all along. I spent at least $2,500.00.

I was well equipped to spend more although I offered she refused after she witness all my check books and credit cards she was informed. I was a man now In my Prime about my money I owed her, she thought how she let me get away. I explain all I ever needed was some one to help me stay out, oppose to someone putting me in Jail. I got a women who act like a women, I care for her because she help me and I help her. She never trying to put me in jail! She kept me out I made money. She knew this women had my heart! She said I can't believe you don't feel for me like you use to? I just put Pete out, I said Pete gonna need you and you gonna need Pete! I can't be with you going through the same thing! The way you just did Pete! I said my women nothing like that! She do exactly as I ask? It keeps us with money. She don't rebel putting me out. We don't argue or fight!

She looked at me, I said now is the time to say remember the rainy day? I said you remember? She said yeah! You said you gonna say to me remember that rainy day? I said can you remember? How I felt when I was in tear? Homeless? the same nigga you just put out stood in the heat, while I was in the rain? See why I say you both need each other! She wanted to cry, although she held back. I ended with I love you! If you can change! I can come home! I love you Max! You are my heart, you always was number one! I chose not to have sex because I respect you that much. I was serious about the Oral; joke! She Replies; I'm not putting that nasty thing you put in her nowhere in my mouth; I laughed! I was serious although joking. I promised that I would make more money. Return home with the kids all she had to do is keep herself up to part.

I notice she was also thinking secondary as if some words were unimportant which I was not going to return back home.

Although I knew when the money was gone. Women change! I told her the truth, we will always be friends and parents of our children! She'll be the number one women in my life forever. I hope it is that way with me! We rubbed hands although we wanted more, we both restrain ourselves. She asked her father what he think I meant explaining what happen! He stated the man seem to love you although, like you found some one else, so have he! He is happy and unwilling to jeopardize his joy! This trip would soon end with pictures as days winded down. We never had made any, I miss you so much love. I guess the mood wasn't correct, although we took photos everyone begin crying, this was just a flight, I assured her whenever you want the kids. I will send them back out too you, give me heads up at-least a months time.

She cried; reaching my heart, I almost canceled the return trip. I pulled off I popped in Nappy roots I played their song, she became even more emotionally distraught. I was quietly wiping away my tears, I was missing her already who knew the 6 months she needed would cost her life? A phone rang! It tore my entire world down! " ring ring ring ring!" Hello! crying in the back ground, a voice echoes; big Ray; Only person call me that is Max? Who is this? Max why you playing on the phone? Big Ray and crying! Stop playing Max! why you doing this? Whats wrong? Big Ray,Max is dead!, Max I know your voice! Why are you playing with me? This is Kizzie, Ray my sister dead! No man, she ain't you, lying! You talking about somebody else! Your information wrong! Call the people. They got the wrong person. It's a mistake she ain't dead! She ain't dead! Have you seen her? Call and ask, look its just mistaken identity! Call me back! I have tell my kids if this! How am I gonna do this? I ain't good with hugs or emotional output! My kids ages 8-7-5 so young how can I do this?

That was one of the bitter moments of my life. Which lead me into a spiral attack of solitude alcohol and PCP abuse. My wife which I married after this incident. She help me get by, although my kids sometimes received artificial love! They suffered more then anybody, due to my wife already having 5 kids which I took care and claim the four, anything else was dead weight or a virus that infects the mainframes. I claim who my heart has emotions for and who had care for us. She did plenty, we struggled with the rivalries which faded soon after I bought boxing gloves. After 4 years the kids were much better with one another, they had dogs,cats,birds,fish 5 cars they receive rides to schools, sometimes they got picked up, I cooked, their stepmother cooked, we ordered out on my check day on Friday's. The wife usually drink Hennessy on my off days, we enjoyed the small ones comedy! My pane continue, although you couldn't see it. I camouflaged my emotion. I begin to feel the death that was now on my clutches.

Crows followed me landing on my Caravan they flew near me. I always knew how to distort the difference, when the silence had transferred, I knew when the birds lingered close, death was some where making preparation. I knew karma was close maybe my time was near? I dreamed of my youngest brother Rob was driving all a sudden, group of guys attempted to shoot him over some female! They argued over nothing, then the dream transformed he was now running and the car hit him! I woke up, fearing for my brother, although I knew it was dreams. I was taking a trip back home to L.A. Although my antennas were Up high I could sense in Chicago, things were Brewing. I was followed, my house was bugged. I mention it seemed as if I was selling Mecca Tons. I had five cars, my measly net pull was at least only 3, 4 ounces a month at least 6,000 dollars I profited, just enough to get broke ass dudes were thinking, especially if they seen your money on the inside, see crimes committed 100% of the time it's people you live with or some who know your secrets! knowing you being plotted against. If you calculate $6,000+1,900+2,500+898=12,000$ sum dollars although this may have been monthly wages. I spent more than I put away!

I figured if you truly ain't got no-one to party with, money and life is boring! I could blow up with my California Connect. Although I stayed low key, I stayed away from getting greedy. I stayed below the big guy radar the fed express. I ain't smart! Although business was sloppy with most dudes, I had dealt. I was train a lot more sophisticated meetings outside was getting me to notice, having 5 cars was suspicious after losing my job. I begin full-time work earning more being unemployed then being employed! I was able to keep tabs on my funds oppose to my secretary whom kept count and drove all the vehicle. She had a compulsive habit of always showing up at her baby daddy house to floss how good and well she was being taking care of the more she showed up he knew sooner he'd have her ass bent over!

This was just a quiet way which it had always been only the outer towner was unaware that the city Chi girl was one of the biggest jail heist bust or breaks he never new what rock-star meant? He was thinking movie star in Chi it meant crack head. I thought hard this chick whom I married background is getting foggy. It seem to be another women behind the persona, her sexual phantasies seem beyond my coping, she seem to have had triples, doubles mini-trains full room orgies! I said damn what in the hell I got myself into? Just like a nigga out of town, meets the fine ass light bright chick all the dudes trying to have sexual relations, after they notice she got but. Then you find out all she got is but! After all the years, you feel if got played, tricked into marrying a prostitute! After your children mothers death, she gave you an ultimatum after the fact! You lose trust, you notice she been chasing after her jelly role shape doughnut boy, whom she had Children by. Now you caught in this sweet as doughnut dipping contest! You decide to spread the seed somewhere else a bit more fertile. Out of three baby fathers one happen to be a Cop! The other Pee-wee Herman with a scooter!

Of coarse the smart one who figure it all out! The so called Husband, married to the nick name call girl, Banana boat! The name earned after boarding the boat, own by a John Wayne, all sorts of orgies, occurred during this activity, rumor was it was just a rumor! The lady who claimed my last name. Supposedly had at-least 9 men in one day! Three at one time, one in the twat, one in the duke and the other in the Pie hole. This is a fact ask her aunt husband son! He shall confirm these acts, he was there! My highlight is this all happened after SEPTEMBER 23, 2008 Man vs machine during this Boating episode occurring during 2009-2010! I was wheel chair captive result of plot-set-up or bad business truth is some shady characters know the facts why?

Notice she has five sons I exclude (one) the oldest who's fathers the Cop. The puzzle never seem to get clearer until I notice my home had been bugged by Crooked Cops in a group whom I was being followed by constantly. The motive is one day the mother the so called wife, took time to visit baby daddy number three whom they share three children, I get a phone call to pick her up, she was unaware that I know how she goes in his room to talk for hours, my kids were my spies, July of 2008 I'm walking unaware that my life would be jeopardize my life 9 years me and the Secretary wife aka Banana Boat is getting old the truth starts to emerge that she was actually a prostitute trying to play house wife. Since she was getting older. I sensed bad habits although I was butmitized, she does have a very huge but. Although she ain't so bright! She have blow jobbed, screwed, nearly an entire Police force her children father whom was supposedly the oldest Son father had a D.N.A test after discovering how stupid she is? He called the marriage off especially after my accident!

They were destined to become a happy couple! Although something happen and changed every thing, he caught her having sex with someone the marriage was called off. Around July, August 2008 the wife and I had big disagreements, I went over board with my feelings actually I felt insulted I wanted her to be real if she was fooling around with dude! All she had to do is admit, I would have pack me my children, my cars, and property. Left her to him, that she feared because if I leave took all my personnel she had nothing but the clothes on her back! This fight started she called to be picked up. I arrive angry knowing how she thought I was foolish. She thought she was jumping in my Ford Expedition as if life was just dandy, everyone knows what baby daddy 3 does in back rooms! thirty minutes.

So I said this chick think I'm a lolly pop. She got up in my truck as soon as she touch the base board. I pulled off smash the gas peddle, she fell out on the ground landing on her but, she hit the ground. I was now in a mind state, they call fools love actually my point was have that nigga drop you off, I timed it to soon because somebody open the back door. I pulled off, she happen to be unlucky, the rear door sent her to the ground if her son had not open the rear door. I would have missed she might have fell although I would have pulled off with just a statement don't go screwing this nigga thinking I'm your taxi man! You got me blank blank up was my attitude! The motive starts here! The executed theories plots begin the bugging of the home some one in the home on September 23, 2008, I was called and informed I had left or either they followed me from home. They needed to make what happen to me look Gang related.

Although I was not Gang related. Especially in Chicago I was a loner I sense and dream this incident Although I was unaware that revenge was being plotted behind the purest motive of Steel vs man occurred on 71 Stewart it was hatched 9752 S. Ewing, 6742 so. Woods These places were wired The Los Angelos Police were Investigating Crimes committed. So they were here to pursue the molestation which occurred with my daughter in California in the foster home all the while they realized the Chicago P.D had me under surveillance some sort of City dispute develop while both force combine to abstract detail, information Then Insults were spoken straight forward toward the L.A.P.D being wimps just like the Crips and Bloods and L.A. is just Hollywood and the Chicago Gangs would destroy L.A gangs and Cops! The Response by L.A was not one Word! A Walk away and some one said check your Stats.

    This was just simple talk in 2006 the Cops who were here decided sense I was giving C.P.D the run around of-coarse I tailgated and played bumper cars with un-mark cars who tailed me. I didn't know who they were, so I chased them. I stop my hustle, the same day they got on my rear. I watch them cut a tree during a storm as it fell on my brand new Cadillac, I had 5 cars 4 worked they were all fast because it was fun loosing them all the time until they G.P.S me. I even start to like the C.P.D style I called them Gangster although with a respect for them being Cops. L.A.P.D just arrested you never new the scamming and scamming they just bust your ass lock you up with 5 million charges and during court if you was on parole you gone for one year behind something made up and lie all you probably did was drive without license and tried to get close to the house so some one could witness in case you might get your ass beat to death or killed.

    When I first arrived I respected how cool it was to see so many black on a Police force. I always said this to the wife she knew how Pro-black I was although I went to my baby mother funeral, tore up so much shit I had even been stop bye the same Cops two days ago, they let me off warned. I said I was from Chicago! I know my city they treat out of town fairly if you are from L.A. Ain't no love. Example things were all good they took the kids from their aunt house, I had to go to the police station to pick them up. We were on our way back home driving. I gave them my name, Social Security number they cared less how my kids just buried their mother! I hold this against L.A Social Workers! They never cared, I lived In Chicago they figure I I got away! They took my kids Illegally due to something happened in Chicago which in Chicago hear say is admissible but in California hearsay get your Kids took, this is the game they played on me. They looked at my California record, that alone I was deemed to be a failing or failure as a man, father you can't father a child you have felonies! I felt so like welcome back to the racist bent laws of L.A. Where the white folks thought I was from Chicago, now they knew I was born here!

    They correcting my pronunciation so I became Chicago

acting ghetto and careless not to kiss their behind they gave me facts and they stipulated my wrap sheet which assault on officer, assault on officer so many other dismissed cases they labeled me by cases dismissed! Except two of them were convictions and they wasn't a cause to take my children! I had been raising, supporting them out of my paycheck for almost a 7 months their mother received funds for them. I didn't ask for one dime! The Family service only cared about my past. I assumed I escaped! They found out I had a Job at that point I had been out of trouble sense 1994 it was now 2004, they didn't care! The people making judgment calls were white and Hispanic.

This why blacks in L.A. are closer then media portray them. Racism is active in gang wars. I got angry when the Social Worker told me I'll have to take Anger management because I spoke up and I was not foolish. I know you were wrong, bias compared to Chicago an Almost pro-black State, whom would have understood how the plotting to get the kids for the money and the lump-some, somehow became motive. Negligent after the baby mothers death. She board a train injured while it derailed it tore her spleen, she was hospitalized treated becoming sickly because of it. The trials I endured due bias acts. The aunt and her father wanted the kids, they knew who ever had the kids would be solely responsible for the money them also. The Social Worker seem be less worried about anything, as if she was more worried about my braids which in California they racial profile braids Indicating Gang affiliation.

They didn't hear me at all! When I spoke, A retard said he don't love his kids if he goes back to Chicago! Leaving them hear. I knew if I stayed my job was gone! After being off work 5 weeks, my job was pulling all they could handle, when I got back I repaid them with doing over time for them on their days. The Social worker check on me every day, and every day I was working! The Judge requested to review my wife children. The Social Worker in Chicago reviewed my wife kids. She found no astounding evidence of abuse! This madness seem to surround ethnicity! The Social Workers of Chicago begin to conflict with the Social Workers in Los Angeles racism was so obvious.

It was hard for blacks to get the good jobs In California!

79

The Hispanic Social Worker assumed blacks were lazy! Until every time she called expect some one other then black to answer the phone, each time she call some one black answered! She was in disbelief what she discovered, she would get the whole truth soon illuminating her bias racist prejudice acts. Without agreeing or compliance she was in denial! I told her that Chicago is predominately Black they knew the deception and poor choice she made. Taking advantage of the situation. She was force to return the kids!

Chapter IX
Deadly Games, Wrong Calls & Bad Decisions

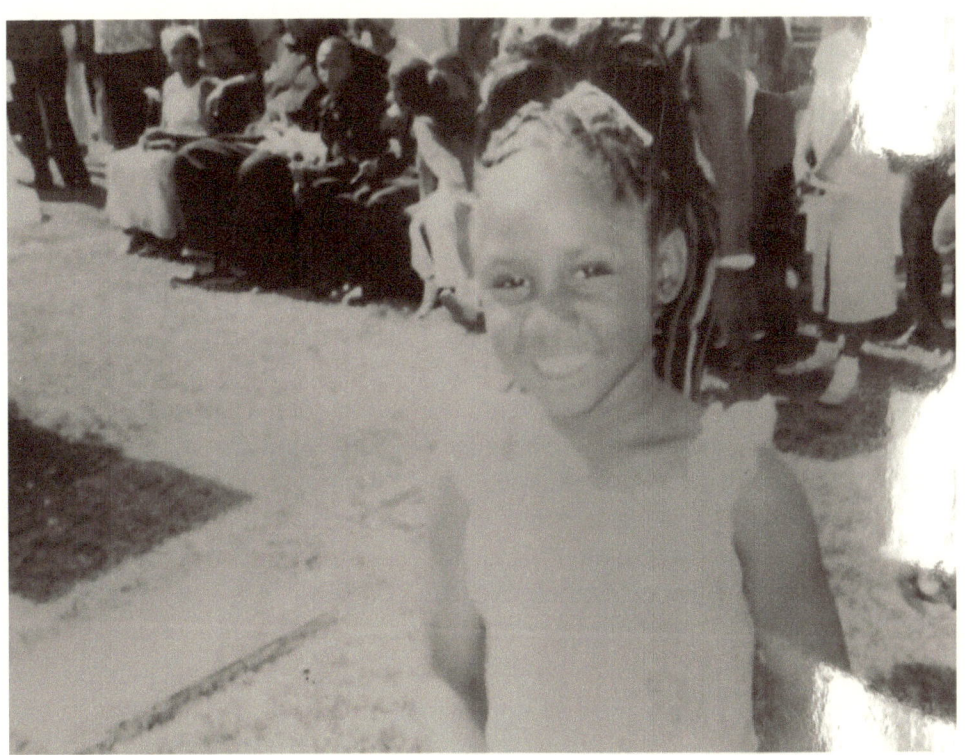

She was instructed to return the children home after hiring so many investigators to find some sort of filth on me! Justifying her actions, she had decided to remove the children with her own appropriate cause, housing them in a home fair and suitable enough to secure their safety Conditions! Which happened to be the worse conditions! My daughter returned home, after the Social Worker of Hispanic descent had been instructed to return them by the Judge personally. He questioned what was her purpose to take Children whom were from out of State visiting? In town to bury their deceased Mother they would never see again! This was insult on top of Injury, which in older age it would define how people care and how bias prejudices along with racial profiling dominating certain people of race ethnicity

Characteristic behavior, unrighteous, unfair, inhuman, choice making! Their school records and residents were located 2,000 miles away. Discovering I was truly employed, married it added insult to injury. She seem so indecisively foolish!

She hired investigators to find any sort of criminal misconduct on me. I lived more then 2 thousand miles away, it would take three days of traveling to pursue me in an high speed car chase! Although plane flights were only four hours! To have face and a nearly ruined reputation she needed evidence of something recent vital with criminal intent. Presented before the courts in order to redeem her name and reputation. She was coerced to take the flight to Chicago meet with the Department of Children family services, whom she had been bickering back and forward with after her reports of Investigating informed her that mostly every place she had to attend were predominately African-American! She was in awe because in California things were so much more different, prejudices racial profiling was at a maximum high, she may have never known she felt a certain way about African-Americans? Until she was surrounded by employed honest working Law Abiding African-Americans! While at the Police station returning my Children, She had a ticket with a Return flight which was immediate and urgent within 2 hours! Which returned her back to California.

I love my State, Although some people I hate with a passion, their prejudices make a place so beautiful so ugly! Misrepresented unfairly! She didn't want to see me nor the Chicago Department Of Children Family Services! Appropriate protocol was to be conducted, I'm not an employee, I figure If they are traveling from another State, they are suppose to Inform make plans to meet with the other States, upon the Children arrival to exchange documents of some sort! Performing a full body cavity search and questions. This Social Worker drop all three children off at the nearest Police station, how ironic? Why? What was her purpose? Was she embarrassed?

Well that cat was out the bag! My kids were home, my daughter at age 8 was very articulate with expressing words and very clear and focus and informative. She said daddy remember um when you said if somebody touch my private part? Um tell you! I said yeah! My baby girl knew I was her protector. I was huge and monstrous to her! No-one could stand before me! She felt safe, my children all knew I was crazy! They knew I would die and kill for them! My daughter waited this long time to break out, as soon as she return, if she couldn't wait for me to topple this pervert? She held her silence so long until she felt comfort, she let it all out! Although she was shy or embarrassed what I would think. I was all she had left as a child. She knew mommie was dead and the only one she could tell was daddy! That she had been violated. What 8 year old child describes in detail what she experienced?

She explained to my new wife whom I assumed I needed the help and I thought it was wise! She did of coarse talk with the child accordingly, the wife and daughter talked for nearly 45minutes I was so full of rage. I went outside smoke two cigarettes, my anger I visioned me on a plane choking the dear life out of her Hispanic foster parents! Who received large sums of money for three foster children, within a four month period enough money to afford a Hummer. My daughter explained how the black teen-age girl was so use to the raping, it was normal, denial was her response! She save my daughter in a sense that she was only 8 years of age! She was the same color, she knew they would most likely experience what she had been through, she would have someone to talk to as well.

She taught my daughter how to hide, my daughter explained in detail so many things which occurred during 4 months that was not documented, some times she would become violent and over the years it effected her so bad That she was suspended every week, she won all her fights and all she fought was boys! Of coarse in our home I taught all the boys to use the punching bag even my daughter and when they had scuffles I made them settle their differences with boxing gloves. They developed an pecking order and respect they annihilated all other kids out doors! Back to the foster home! Although I tried to send help to get the teen age girl out she was to far ahead and ashamed, immune to being raped, her life in adult hood would be ruined! So she denied the raping and abuse, her mental thought of sometimes liking the feeling confusing her of wright or wrong, it happen so much it became normal to her ability to rationalize as she was repeatedly molested no-one came to her rescue! When the Hispanic Social worker rarely asked questions?

Who knows how this teen age girl viewed herself while living with a different race? Who really didn't understand her ethnicity? Abuse, including all the mayhem and racial wars everyone were taking sides even Hispanic Social Workers and Foster parents? Whom caught news that some Black gangs killed 6 Hispanics in a race war, that targets skin color? She was forced to remain silent by her foster parents, even the mom forced her to not say a word, how sick the wife was she had to know of her husband acts and deeds! She remained hush silent she was just as guilty. We took my daughter to the nearest hospital at St. Bernard. She was examined, the doctor confirmed her hymen was pushed in, she was violated at age 8 year of age!

I wanted to catch a Plane and play the game of swords off with your head! My daughter talked with the doctor very long, he called California! He called the hotline, and Chicago Family services they documented the new editions of abuse into evidence, after I begin filing an lawsuit against the State Of California in behalf of my daughter! These crooks went after me and my profile in L.A. They sent dozens of investigators to Chicago and some how with law Illegal or legal the bugged my cars and home with the help of Chicago P.D. In the year 2006. My daughter case was extremely strong. Although my attorney was weak broken by the prejudices of impressing whites in California. she seem as if she had some kind of alcohol addiction of some sort! I was paying her to start $500.00 and two to three hundred here and there until the case was settled.

This case was so strong my attorney sold me out for a price in covert. As they all due when such cases fall apart against the State oppose to paying you they pay the attorneys representing you to lose your files and Pete Rose or forget the game plan. With a flop or Phantom punch! I am unaware although, she was approached, they had discovered things about me, that were profound and confidential! I wanted to pull their bluff although my attorney was attempting to bail out at that point. I knew she had been compromised, while she was encouraging me in court the good thing we won! The Judge found negligence involved, okay now my daughter is eligible to be rewarded for pane and stress insult on top of long term emotional injury after the fact of losing her mother needing fatherly consoling and this bastard debated an plotted out when to molest her the State of California! Rather invest in a game of you are going up against deep pockets, me being African-American and male!

With a long California record and a very Dark past! I knew things were going to be bad for me representing as Guardian of my daughter. Although it was about my daughter being the victim! The deposition they tricked my daughter up with trick questions to confuse a child! Although her story was the same she may have added thoughts she remembered over a four month period details become novels! They said; oh the story have change! I said; of coarse she remembers many details it wasn't something which happen one day, she lived their for quite some while, so things she forgot were now enlightened. They even seek out what I had done in the past oppose to what happen to my daughter! During their judgment call to sabotage the decisions. Determining if where she was housed was more secure then her living with me? She was abducted similar to how slaves were separated forced to live somewhere supposedly stable considered loving, caring, and safe! The spoke of this family as if they were so innocent and they had never been in such a big lie, they tried to make it as if my daughter was just a habitual liar. I said the doctor evidence don't lie. The Social Worker alibi was she has 5 step brothers. The story told By the Social Worker that she was humping on the younger 4 year old Step brother!

I said it seems the truth is becoming more like prejudices! I know if my daughter name was Sarah, she would be the pure innocent white child with no harm or no wrong which would be permitted her rewarded for abuse and so forth! Although as a 8 year old child with three people in one room her words seems to be invalid when her story never changing about what he done! I watched her emotionally distraught and breakdown at home, speaking how no boy will ever like her screaming, I hate him! I hate Him! This was the essence of my daughter. Beyond their watch of coarse they were white and caring as-well as concern was out of the story! She indicated it was all about a payment she was correct it was about suffering and pane similar to when a white ladies spills coffee in her lap she sues and wins millions? Black girls raped, molested, regularly in foster homes not one case is rewarded a benefit or one penny! I sat in a room reminded in California how real the racism is, they act and expect the Blacks to brown nose, if you want anything.

The Gangs had begin to target their white communities taking their children college funds so they decided to make harsh laws for home invasions! The hood stars were going out hitting targets and scoring hundreds of thousands in cash and jewelry in a heist when two thugs keep hush hush and split 300 thousand down the middle they usually invest and triple what they gained and even spread the wealth, this was why most black politicians were being framed force to retire until all seats were occupied by mostly all whites. Although Maxine Waters had a seat she kept a crowd of intellectual protesting ready and firm blacks in her circle, they were doctors educated ex-gang counselors lawyers and so forth. The one thing that plagued California was the Surenos and their belief in hating blacks! Being pure racist and breeding the hate into their children.

Despite losing the case or being sold out, I assumed one

day America would Repay my children 10 fold for their wrongs! After their mothers death, If they been any other color they would have received the inheritance of the train and the negligence and sexual abuse. My kids should be millionaires by the age of 18 years old! They were suppose to be set for life financially! I did all I could, I was 27 years old and my convictions plagued their decisions, I was the remaining living parent! The courts did all they could to prevent a black child from reaping the spoils of a true event and action of violations! I wonder If they write out checks of apologies and finding redemption seeking to reimburse families on trains that derailed and children whom were in foster care and abused my kids would become suddenly fitly rich?

<u>Chapter X</u>
The Good, The Bad, The Ugly,
Man Vs. Steel And Lives

September 23, 2008, I was mowed down like cutting grass the vehicle was my 1998 Ford Expedition this 2-ton weapon had broken 10 ribs,femur,contorted both legs the opposite direction I had to have both legs broke in surgery my right hip was artificially replaced with a plate my skull was fractured, I had swelling on the brain, a broken left arm from being shot with nerve damage in my arm and even my entire body suffered nerve damage and broken or fractured bones they turned me into the MAN OF STEEL!

Rods were everywhere my legs, my spine my right arm, my left hip. This accident would have killed 999 out of a thousand! The average men couldn't have lived or endured the torturing pane I insulted my assailants for being cowards and preparing for one man as if they were approaching Optimus Prime or an small army it took so many men to orchestrate a plan to annihilate an unarmed man in my younger years in such a situation I would have been the lone ranger knowing he was unarmed a tooth pick would have been just as lethal then 5 cars ten assailants crooked ass cops and sprinkled with some street punks! This so called carjacking was actually a premeditated event that had been a product of some Good guys gone bad. You see well after California had left and decided there was nothing further to pursue.

2006-2008 While C.P.D continued to observe my every move. They watch me have sexual relations with my wife, they made comments out loud in the public verifying they were violating my wrights! I decided if the fags wanted to watch penis I entertained the Camera, even the Women who were getting 30 minutes at home, they worked next to their lovers on the job. Cameras filmed me and the wife. I carried on my sessions for many long hours. They took lunch breaks, returned, I was still in pound mode. Which I don't ease up off the peddle the Wife will attest to that true fact! Oh Tish I had to mention you!

The Cop Women nick named me the energizer rabbit. I nicknamed myself the California kid on camera! When I would display a two hour freak session the female Cops got hot while I forced my wife to say who p**** is this? I would say Say California! I said to them looking at the location of the Cameras! If you got erectile dysfunctions send your wife to me. I'll fix her back and her 3-minute problem. I knew these niggers would be mad. I was insulting them drinking and smoking and feeling good as well! I became obnoxious as my privacy was invaded, saying things I knew that would push them over the edge intentionally! I talked about how the Crips and Bloods were always anointed the best and always the engineers why the word Gang Capitol existed! I talked how prehistoric their police force is whom was controlled and operated by gangs. I said how the L.A.P.D had so much training thanks to California Gangs they were sent to every state to train the less organized cities who was over run by gangs!

They thought I was joking the City of Chicago gang violence Increased! You know who they called to crack down on the crime, The Federal Cops, mostly all promoted and from California. Instructing them how to conduct themselves, they were outrage how I had said things they researched and became embarrassed to know what they assumed was dangerous was just undermined in the placed they lived. It couldn't be a city outside of Chicago just as dangerous? Is what they were thinking! Violence was simple to people who lived elsewhere and endured worse! The knew Cops bragged so much about the place they fought gangs and how much more dangerous they were in the 1990's the Chicago P.D grew angry and envious of California. The knew Cops enforced the streets of Chicago to give them An example, they noticed how corrupt the sickness was they begin to report that the city would need a purging the hate was spilling every where!

The Cops from California were as they say to cocky, after the Certain California investigators return back to their State. They contacted the Bureau to Inform them how infested with crime the entire State was and they would need the big shabang. My point is crime dropped and the Bureau continue to occupy

Chicago in year 2014! So you see I live because I am some what if you would say special! They meaning Chicago P.D Know the reality, they have attempted sending Pawns, although the Pawns were intercepted any one claiming they are from Illinois. Now is scrutinized and thoroughly researched before occupying in other fields in Politicians, it would seem all this happen after my attack and the people involved who was angry how they were embarrassed by Law enforcement from out of town they waited until they returned back to their State and the out of towner said if you having trouble and such a hard time you deal with him we will drop our charges!

This is how I became the sole target of the so called carjacking! My city the motive for embarrassing certain Cops on all angles the Range and in the fields of their own city! Now 2014 so many crooked cops are now inspired full time drug dealers after being sniffed out and fired after my accident they figured they would say look what our city gangs done to your so called hard core L.A Gang banger! I survived and they knew if I was to put the pieces together and the correct people figured it out hell would break loose! The new Cops sort to say, had too much respect for their State and city to watch and let some weak knees cowards spit in their cities face even as a criminal I was treated like dirt in so many words this was the covert message to the Out of towners! It wasn't about race it was about principalities and the battering ram went to work the citizens don't know this but this is why the media is always saying the murder rate is so high! This is why they keep offering to bring in the National Guard and Army train and are base mostly in California things go bad they pull out the big boys to settle cities enraged!

In the state of California near Area 51 bombs have been launched in the many deserts! This is what C.P.D didn't expect! They illegally spied on me 2006 oppose to all the Chicago born bad guys C.P.D. was interested in watching me have sex how corny! I gave her my deadly death strokes and I said say when you nutting! They listened, they counted 1-2-3-4-5-6 and they were awe saying damn, he still going, machine in motion was my motto I said it repeatedly until they became discussed. I begin talking to the camera and pleasing the wife a swell while smoking a Newport and drinking my vodka all while in motion. My second wind kicked in giving me three hours of exercise. Two hours was the usual I normally attempted to go more if she allowed, of course this was the wife!

These bastards became Infatuated and made side offers this is how she became the Crooked Police Department(CPD) whore, she prostituted and screwed quite a few while she, had been considered suspect in my case. They used wits and reverse psychology to get free ass, until they grew tired of her orchestrated as pissing me off was Cop motive. This is raw truth, although cold hearts and authentic 2010 they informed the wife after they had did all they had done to violating her not to see me anymore! She got a check she invited my kids and me to eat at Old Country Buffet I been paralyzed 2 years at this point, the wife returned back to assist me 2009 due to the guilty countenance of knowing and being involved, one day I dropped her off at her aunt house Natalie! Where she moved back 2010, she said after Monday I can't see you or work for you anymore! I was curious why not?

She even hinted you need to move back home, I knew she was held against wanting to go along after returning back after a year and knowing when I pulled off it was pure emotions and now the people she was acquainted with owned her. They convinced her it was all her fault if they go down she had to pay or confess! She was also my caregiver, after she stop showing up, the heat was on! My house was vandalized bugged it sounded like a field of telephone lines if you turned of the TV. 2010 until 2014 I have probably seen her five times since she was instructed not to see me anymore! After eating at the buffet this meant my kids also were off limits. Somehow she developed a true love for my two younger Children as a mother. My kids strangely grew to love her.

I knew she made a terrible mistake for not speaking openly and saying that man made a mistake he was upset and I know I was doing wrong insulting his intelligence, that much I do respect her for being their and helping the kids When I wasn't able. Due to intense surveillance and harassment she knew! I knew some one was attempting to finish this incomplete job so did she. She begin to care trying to use the kids to get me out of this City.

My macho bravado would not allow me to leave. I stated they gotta kill me before they make me run again! I had decided death was more important then living like a coward! I rather had died once, then die a coward a million times, the way the idiots involved would have to live after all I was still in a wheel chair I drove like a maniac despite what they done especially after noticing they followed me again. The chase was still on. The ones who did me in realized I wouldn't average seem to have a death wish. It wasn't that I just never settled to being a carpet are rolling out carpet to no one! If I was going to die, I rather the coward as crooked Cops came out to face me! When they planted The duffel bag Full of Guns on me? They followed me in my 1974 Buick Century which had been completely restored it had 22" tires white burgundy leather, I put it in storage on 95 at Smart Stop Storage.

Someone mysteriously broke in to the storage choosing my vehicle out of all cars! Some were more fancier then mine and even older with 24"tires, they attempted to steal my tires check the records how many cars were insured and had rims? They failed to steal the rims, so they scratched the paint! A few months later the set it on complete fire with a cock tail and I paid insurance although once again the State robbed me again. these are reasons which I consider selling drugs making up for all the negligence and discrimination as a drug dealer these reasons made me buy and sell 5 -8 ounces! Believe it or not all people of race go through these types of rip offs until they are nearly bankrupt. Certain lawsuits get bought out by your own lawyers who get paid off to lose your files. So the rescue is the hustle! I lost an total restored America muscle Car!

My passion! You know how it goes fast cars, even faster

women, fast money. If I said the other one, ill be indicted in my ongoing case as guilty! Confessing, Although I was framed! This is all in Police documents my vehicles' vandalism – both Ford Expedition and Buick Century, my tire were flattened at least 7 times, my four windows were broke separately! I was seriously being harassed to be frightened to run and hide! I was even unarmed and crippled.

They used the same guys who ran me over to follow me all the way to Indiana, and send these messages. They vandalized my home and the police I called to have a report, told me to go to home depot? Home depot? Home depot? I feared for my family one day I notice they were following me! I pulled up at the police station on 18 street after driving as far as from 9752 S. Ewing. The cops there told me to go to the nearest Police station near my Home! I said you don't understand the guys who paralyzed me are outside! He responded well go to the Police station near your home! I went to their bathroom and someone whom happen to be a Cop yelled out, "You diaper wearing Son Of A Bitch!" I then realized the crooks who was following me were also Inside!

At that point I knew they had bugged my home, this rabbit hole was much deeper then my judge who is in charge of my case could assume! He got the wrong one! The difference between a Cop and a Crook One got caught and the other one didn't! They were watching my home and invading my privacy. It was almost two years of being paralyzed. I hadn't learn to control my body function! Although then I was down and out. I can't embarrass them completely, how I could if I was walking. They exploited my crippling situation!

By having sexual relations with my ex-wife, saying things in public tipping me off, somehow they placed a device in my home. So I could hear my wife moan and groan while I was crippled still effected. I was unable to have sex and I couldn't move like when I was walking. This was insulting. I heard her voice she even attempted to block them out from trying to insult me! If they screwed her, she knew them, they knew me and what happened to me! They knew I read between lines very good, after all I seen them before they even begin investigating me!

I quit hustling and they had nothing but my clients calling

95

me two years later! I was intended as dead! I survived! I am in a wheel chair, they continue to stalk me! I continue to call them Cowards and they even intended to have me arrested! Planting a duffel bag full of large caliber weapons and 10 boxes of bullets which they intended to lock me away with this plot! As well, sense they couldn't finish the job! I learned when I took my family to the 18 street police station! They were no good and there was no help after explaining to them how I was pursued and the same suspects, who did this is outside pointing to my chair! He looked at me like who give a fuck? I wanted to shoot that Cop in the face so bad!!!!!!! Although I was unarmed, I didn't even have a butter knife! I started reading the bible and begin to forget and forgive, well the truth I tried to forget the forgiving part is all up to God! Sometime I flashback after a dream. I became depressed, I suppressed my anger until no-one would help me or my family and all the Cops were worse then the bad Guys!

The moral of the story is the good, the bad, the ugly is true facts events and puzzle pieces 2014! They are trying to convict me for a bag of planted guns, while Crooked ass Cops walk freely! I wonder how high up is this sort of corruption? We all know about the Politicians in Chicago! What that explains about the Police? If I am convicted sent to their Jails, I'll never make it out! These crooked Cops planned this so it would leave no trail or evidence, now it does! As I said, I see with foresight, I see a plot designed, hatching beforehand, this one has been brewed since 2013 Dec 8 they arrested me! I been planning to write about this conspiracy sense 2010! They promised to leave me be! and backed away, they broke that promise and code just like Cops!

I break my silence! My ink is my weapons, some Cops kill ending you with bullets! Attempting to take your life! I found out how to end them, with ink the same way they write false police reports, truth and strong forceful words and description this is similar to Cops knowing the show is over, it's curtains facts are, all in the streets and the people who can take back their rights! The crooked Cops are rendered, with two choices being guilty and manning up or taking their cowardly way out loading up squeezing their throw-away 38 special pulling the trigger and committing mass hysteria alarming numbers of suicides! Similar to the movie American Gangster! That's just fine with me! That's called American justice and the power of Inc. Does Inc murder? Or is it the writer?

I'm quite curious about the guy the wife call her friend as she says to me! Although on Facebook, she says her lover? He seem to be an C.P. D implant/heroin attic sent and paid to monitor her to keep tabs, thus how vital she is how many faces she's seen. She is a vital chess piece! Her and how much evidence is inside her wound, due to sexual relations. She is vital and pressure break pipes! I know her! She once told me, "I don't watch because what I don't see, I can't say." This indicates the faces she seen, if questioned, she will give full detail, dates, times, numbers, and prices even addresses! Some names are mention to set free those men, women who were victims to crimes by such a group of misfits, even if some people who were targets couldn't even call a single honest Cop!

I hope the judge involved to review me begin to review these crooked Cops who framed me and threatened my family lives starting from2006- 2008! actually search for my entire family even in California, ask them if they have had any contact with anyone from Chicago? That rescues my case! I Attempt to save the unheard voice less, victims who no one heard, their screams and cries, while they were tortured! No one believed or helped them or their own families were even murdered! Before their very own eyes being tortured and knowing you going to die, is traumatic and hard to cope with, either you will well protect yourselves or become a victim repeatedly in such a State where fighting crime fails and being rogue is law! Although double standers apply you keep quiet they treat you like some two dollar whore, ask my ex-wife?

The moral is she has three children fathers the Cop? The first! Peewee-Herman the scooter bike, beep-beep stay the hell out, what his baby mother involved in! He would lock her ass outside not answering the door bell! Before he went out like Super-Dave! saving the Poo-nannie, Baby dad #3 Fat-boy Jelly Doughnut, he smarter then the average bear after realizing how many pawns and fools were involved in her Older sons plan to save his own Cowardly ass!

When I spooked him knowing he didn't know bleep about crime, this was 2010! They bugged my home thanks to the son father number one? Who allowed his Cop Equipment and policed connect to single me out! September 23 2008 when I was mowed down car jacked. Two years later the son was sitting in my living room! He had dreads then, my children open the doors, he fake the role big brother, he manipulated the dog sh**t out of my youngest son after I told them both to never let him in. They always thought it was a joke. Even while they opened the door when his mother was with me. I informed her when ever her son visits he had to sit outside! So while he was at my house while his mother moved out 2010. He had no business at my home!

When I said he was involved now my daughter is 18 years old. She know more about reality! Although she also can put away many perpetrators. Every sense I seen him sitting on my couch in my house uninvited! Aware I sent his momma a text, which was bait! Who ever mother son was involved, will be canceling all birthday candles and birthdays! I made sure she seen a big fake be-be gun. I painted all black, I bought from Wal-Mart. I knew if she was involved she was informed to deliver detail, I assume she said Roy you better be careful if you see Ray, I think he know you set him up to be paralyzed! He would respond what he going to do in a wheel chair? He can't even move to see me when I'm running through his own house? He easy if I wanted to get him all I gotta do is sneak up on him! Why he sleep and have his kids open the door, but ill make it look like poison or something!

She says; I seen His new gun, he say what kind of Gun he got? She say the one with the long big curve clip, he says shit he ain't playing, he gotta a chopper. He says I better get something case this fool pull something! She say stop playing Roy, people in wheel chairs can get you when you least expect! Putting your guards down stop sneaking in that man house! Playing games with him, he say's I know he got some money! Now my legs gone, his heart grows enormous! The father who is the cop makes the biggest mistake of his Muslim life! Being involved with people who exterminate their African race!

Number two mistake, Having sexual relation with another

man wife, the karma returned he discovered in his sexual relation with his baby mother how far she allowed lies to develop and grow. She didn't even attempt to prevent an event which could go bad! They mentioned she better have insurance, she thought they were all business, she fell full fledged with out a doubt. She did as she was informed, money was issued for no purpose. All the funny money was marked, they would use it later when the heat got hot to get her with you can go to jail or you can give all us some ass! They called baby daddy number 1 a punk! He seen all the mee-lay he said look this is on you and him, I can't sell out like this!

This was 2010 the accident already occurred and the son was so afraid. I lived to testify in court, he would lose his career in karate! He was influence that attempt murder carries 25 years of coarse I said that to keep him jittery and nervous. I could hear him from upstairs in the vacated, supposedly empty apartment. They now occupied, the landlord is a good I witness. The pipes in the house echoed, where they had their loud beeping equipment! I could hear them talking clear while they were listening and talking asking why I wasn't moving! While I pretend to be possum wondering why I heard people discussing talk such as he look better! Can he walk now? They said they had police decoder that kept them from being detected by body scan or thermos, heat motion detectors? I wondered how they knew so much about my condition. I tuned in, I noticed my wife's and son's voices after they discovered, I could hear them they begin to whisper! I knew they had cameras also.

Although I notice how I heard hood fellas a female or two who were being exposed as front line informants. Once this little birdie and the design hatched this blows down the farm factory! Exposing who ever step forward and whom ever don't because so many details, I knew from always having some one trying to locate my where about? If I don't get home to California or not that's why it may have been attempts to expand the numbers of so called dying certificates! Sign your name on the line you black you good as gone deceased! Just scare tactics to keep me quiet. Although I was never afraid just living by street silence and pride not anymore! I see ain't no rules and even, Thugs going along to get me arrested or missing!

Ready to tell, they used mere delusion of traffic increase numbers when you are afraid and impersonation along with lies of breaking the law, if you don't allow us to survey this, they use many quick lies. You should ask for badge numbers and warrants signed by judges and the State Attorney and legal numbers! Even get something with their finger prints see how fast they vanish! Ask to pluck their hair to keep their DNA! Don't be fooled by fake Cops Impersonation! If they decide to get gangster! My Carjacking is connected to J-Hud family crimes! The perp in Prison didn't operate alone. Too much technology and Police equipment is being used, not many drug dealers can call the Police. To report someone, while somebody listened in on their phone calls! Ripped off and stole their biggest drug quantities! This is what this group have been connected to. Does it define everyone involved becoming expendable? You ask where's my proof?

I was a ex-gang affiliate and dealer that's my evidence! We know what the media leaves out and through out years the streets have a tell tell. I got a reputation bragging wrights of who done what! With the credentials of a scholar, check my leads! Don't back out watch the cookie crumble! Connect my dots this is how crimes are solved? If most of these people ain't already missing it equals M.D.K. I high light my family that is because they may have been approached? I was not afraid to die and spoke out loud how I would bring their corporate fag farm down to their smelly pink panties! Lets play connect four. The wife son and his buddies Marlin and Tony although Marlin and unknown assailant were murdered three weeks after Marlin said what up Ray? He seem discussed with Stevon as he called him!

Unlike his mother who calls him Roy! Marlin seem angry with the mention of the name, he reminisce of the old days. Although he seemed effected with something that seem to go bad, he assume approaching me it would keep him on record! After all his best friend is how we knew each other! If some one had been involved with a blessing, the other was someone left behind like old news! Almost like a friend gone rogue, who begin to hang with a more popular crew and completely brushed off his child hood friends! Marlin and Tony, he said he change sense he got that money? Indicating Stavone, as he called him.

I was curious, I said what money? Because I heard his mother was dating cops, to pay her rent! I knew that the fights he had barely even earned anything close to two or three thousand dollars! With all the fees deducted which had to be paid of coarse amateur fighters don't earn no chips! They may fight once every 4-6 months even longer. That's why they get involved in other trades. I knew Marlin was reaching out at me for a reason, he even mentioned where he lived, above the store on commercial! He explained how he had disdain how Stavon think that karate can save him, he use it like a bully! I said oh yeah? He said you cool Ray! You can kick at my house over their anytime! I just nodded saying okay, although I didn't trust him or anything he was speaking, until he got dead. I called Stavon mother to inform her sense she reports everything she see or hear to her son, or those who employ them both! I said you remember Marlin your son friend? She says no!

I thought, *how suspicious?* If she knew about some sort of plot or threat beforehand! If someone was red flagged. I guess she assumed I was going to say he dead! I only said, "I seen him just now! He was over our house every day!" Trying to get his so-called best friend he called messy Marvin to do what was correct. When she denied knowing him, it raised my radar! Although I continue to say he say your son head to big for some reason! He don't know his friends sense he move on down what ever it may have meant? Although three weeks down the line Marlin allowed a friend in which he knew inside his apt/home on commercial and him and another assailant were killed over some electronic device. Immediately I had a clue it was Marlin! I seen it reported on news! These are all clues that are puzzles pieces who knows who and connect the dots? I know my wife son wasn't the person who ran me over. Although he wanted take full responsibility after his mother put a 10 on a 2 over exaggerating how she was run over with so much attention, she never felt this appreciated or important by pure strangers! She couldn't deny the effect which caused me just as they plan not to hurt me to bad!

The wife may have forgotten about the incidents and her

child wanted to prove that he wasn't just a fighter, something about the gun which disqualified the kung fu useless and these dudes with guns would have ended him in a heart beat blink! It was her son he excited this frenzy mob September 2008, he told them how much money he thought I had after always knowing me to spend 4,000 dollars on fire works and breaking in the home once accumulating 1,500 dollar while I was in a bind also observing his mother tend and collect all my money begging, his mother refused stating, "This Ray money, he became a parasite!"

I hadn't hustle in nearly months they assumed I was big balling after they also targeted Eric 2008 it went haywire they dropped the gun. Although the motive is similar in all three violent events. I mention it occurs in the same neighborhood, how ironic is that? They followed Eric to his mother house, he was a hustler! My adopted aunt told me the locals were inquiring if me and Eric had been serving Heroin? The 69 Perry location they are all connected Ikeem is connected to Stavon and I keem grew up on Perry and 69 he hangs where Jhud family was massacred check his wrap sheet! Weeks later Eric was robbed!

Three weeks after him, I was followed and not so fortunate. My wife son is the same bastard who set on my couch and tried to trick my children into poisoning me since, I survived and no insurance money was being issued! This was 2009 almost 2010. This same coward visited me in the Renaissance nursing home 2008, his mother brought him, he couldn't look at me eye to eye! I knew this pussy cat female mommies boy born as coward. Couldn't stare in my eyes. I knew day one to place him on my list of who was the responsible crew. I know Ikeem my ex landlord Thurman Warmack son notice me, he passed the gun to someone else. Although he was at my adapted aunt house two weeks before my incident!

So I started this string of connect the dots, the ex-wife was hurt. The son father had cop connection and ability to have walkies talkies, camera, and motion detector decoders phone and computer scramblers. The wife son went to school at Robeson high with ikeem, Tony, Marlin and few more fellows. The fellows who dealt with J-hud family are the same crew of stick up artist involved in the other 2 events. If J-hud brother was considered to have large amounts of money! He became a target while not getting out of the hood with a famous sister he might have flossed too much money around voltures who knew he would gain even more. Envy killed him! The scout was the boyfriend the inside guy who delivered what he knew to a crew. He was attempting to prove himself. The cowards were very young and acted on impulse the hood always knows the truth!

The police or correct police ain't work harder enough. They are settled with the ponzy! In my situation the scout was ikeem from the same area where J-hud relatives were finished. Simply ask where was the sister? She was no where near? Why the boy was took out the house? Balfour didn't work alone! The answers continue to be in his hood. He is so called staying gangster, the fact is he wont hold out too long. Some one in jail know every detail there is especially after he discovered, he been had, they attempting to sleep with his money, his girl! Just sooner or later he will be looking for a deal for reduced time, that is after he realized they trying to target him from prison attacking and threatening his family. Depends on how ranked he is if it work? Although the cowards who killed the little boy continue to be on the street! Well my point they ain't arrested no-one for the first two murders, well after either the plan fell apart after some one unanimously called the cops? How long were the family hostage? Before they were murdered? 71 Stewart this string of Robberies are connected and many more.

I recall a older man who sold P.C.P I seen him being escorted around with some one, he claimed was his nephew, he seem to be a tax collector from around the area of 71 although, I don't know what happen with the Old fella? I know these cowards turn simple robberies into unnecessary murders! Ware the damn mask! The dead speak from the grave! Do you hear them in ink? Saying connect the crimes. If the Cops don't know they ain't all good. Its a more uglier bad situation. If they ain't brought out or sold out, the pieces of the hood, the crimes committed with similarities of holding hostages longer then 5 minutes, each crook trying to out bravado the next while crimes pile up! The names of perpetration who orchestrated may now be involved affiliation.

My word and my witnessing someone in my home who

was not welcome indicated he had something to do with my situation! His biggest mistake was letting me see his face! Thinking he was a damn ninja. The crazy shit boogeyman, I am the devil, shit ain't working, dead bodies exist with J-hud 2 years after this crew was established... I know for a fact despite the clean record and kung-fu your mind and hands or dirty, you hear me lil ass pussy cat? You scared to do time in a room confined forever, knowing the Cops had you wired up ask Ikeem he knows? You got some big timers in jail, they thought Steven Roy was with the business? He played two sides of the fence, remember the Cops? Know how fast you will turn state evidence. Just like I know? This why I decided to put this out oppose to you calling and you remember informing the Chicago P.D. who didn't trust you then? I'm sure they know how you tried to force your mother to say she heard me confess to murders and how many people I killed? When I told her war stories. You never understood I told her the life I lived the way and how dangerous California was and how the Feds cleaned it up! How I had killed coward ass niggas in my mind a million times especially after my accident my dreams were all death and horrifying even now!

Although I explain the same way my books explains that the life was deadly and take no one for hostage, don't take or turn simple foolishness robberies into life sentences! She was never a witness because she is From Chicago I'm from California! She think red and blue mean war? I knew this was a heist pretend crooked volunteer Cops and crooks sticking up specific so call drug dealers In Chicago, I had seen this sort of crime develop directly before my eyes in California!, J-hud family was victimized, although the click assumed they were going to eat good playing monopoly. I seen your face in a location you were not meant to be the day my kids confess you was there, your done and what happen to the chick? We getting money playing the drake song? Names such as Robert Coleman, C-greenfield, D-greenfield are Important, that is if this small crew used Chicago P.d and J. Edgar Hoover tapping device to seem more then they are. Same tactics I used with spray paint! Seem greater in numbers with broader outreach! Recording devices can be purchased even bugs!

Just like American Gangster, how can a fool attempt what has already been done although every fool meets their same folly! 10 years is what Fed X always give you. When they nail you assuming, I thought we was connected? Fool we was undercover! Who is the undercover guy? They may have traveled to California perpetrating in progress. I mention mediate family on paper we all keep us on radar. I rewarded no one points because they can't hush me up or set me up. They almost had me! If the script fit prepare yourselves, your life is better then someone trying to get yours! I'm writing this very strange documented detail of my carjacking, the people who are involved one day, they can be question, this truth will sit with their resumes! If they try to walk away sky free from other events, that may have even occurred. I mention Tisha she was a good friend and the people at 410 Bowen whom seek to put forward good agendas although, Now they know they were being mislead to cover up what happen in J Hud home!

That was just one incident, while the few continue to target victims now you see how important I'm and what I discovered with connecting my own dots. So I write for the boy who is voiceless thanks to a man who feared jail like a coward. He chose to kill the boy! Suppose to the fear he had of being caught, which meant he feared time doing crimes was simple. Killing a boy indicating he can't do no time! So this profiles someone who never been to prison. Convicts ware mask and plan carefully to not get caught and minimum amount of damage is committed. Compared to this never been a inmate. This perpetrator was building, craving, wanting to repair an stripped reputation, some one destroyed him this type of killing built his reputation as a coward. He was with a crew and crew members established unspeakable crimes under their belts, this begin as tell tale signs of sloppiness no-one would have been killed if they brought along a stranger and a mask! They were rookies, they hide when it's chill, hide hot. They go out of town 6 months or less, visiting different Continent is the best Alibi.

My purpose is to get the ball rolling and get these true clowns removed! I am not with black on black, although I have bully annihilation with intent. I know cold blooded stone Killers!

These dudes had stripes like Predator, killing ,Alien, killing Jason, Killing Freddy, Killing, Michael Myers when I say I don't talk just to hear me. They would have been so smooth senseless murders would have been prevented and the coldest tough guy like a baby face nelson for example or Al-Capone are people they target mot armless old ladies and little boys who don't grow up because you seen my face and they probably forgot after staring at the gun. These were video game killers kids trying to be proved! Any coward who kill someone harmless although he fears the old way barrel to barrel one stand one dies!

When God ain't with you, then you are numbered! Not even your alligator tooth or rabbit foot can save you! Back to life I was bless in death to see a side unknown, almost to say my attackers were a blessing. I write for the sleepwalker in which the individuals are whom were involved in my situation. They are in fear and continue to keep tabs in order to protect their corporate drug line venue. What they do once, I'm writing showing motive! If they make one move toward me! Although I'm unafraid, they know how they have even attempted to frame me with a bag of weapons and this case is open as we speak! Being a new change regular mature citizen paying taxes and being touched spiritually with a divine intervention. The courts know how some cop drug payoff cut is being interfered with! The good, the bad, the ugly. Now they wonder why they have not been able to finish me off?

My belief and faith in God how he has protected a guided and shielded me from destruction allowing me to introduce my monumental views of point and how I'm able to write delivering truths from the grave. My talent was having one foot in one foot out. I write its like the deceased is giving me details to piece together cases unsolved as the dead has a story, they speak in ink, dead men have always had a tale some never had an entrepreneur to help solve their senseless crimes and the law of the world is to provide evidence. I connected the dots now all is needed is foot work. I promise so many bodies or going to emerge like the wire. in the abandoned buildings. I just need a loyal trustworthy cop unwilling, unmoved, untouched, untainted, to come out like me and not be brought out!

My pride is more valuable then any billions offered! No

money can substitute the blankness of a stolen life! I ain't the snitch! I also ain't the fool or disciple to follow a group or their purpose! I set trends! I make my way, now my knew found way cowards who want to imitate televisions scarred of doing time! I have profiled these crack babies of the eighties, they watched some movie and decided to build personalities of a monster created to strike fear. I'm busting their bubble a punk will emerge. The very first time they were not comfortable now they think they are untouchable so did Al-Capone you filthy dirty black bastards your skin color is your guilt, you will never go untouched innocently protected riding off in the sunset freely while targeting black folk! I will bring you down and white folks aren't Jeopardizing a foolish Negro to pull down and corrupt the law any further with unprofessional senseless acts that forever illuminating with prints and voices from the grave, speaking out loud connect the pieces.

The true suspect are still at work accumulating more senseless acts! This is my purpose history and a monumental spot as I survived so much I' am ordained to do things in a way which the messengers of above utilizes my talents. I have just begin my testimonies of survival explaining How God pulled me from the wrath of death and not miracle my foolishness and gang ties along with gun hoe brushes with death. I'm not afraid to expose or write stories about anyone my amends are what urges me! Indulging in a gang affiliation, I never had intent to target innocent people. I always wanted the people who killed innocent children and women intentionally, they were the ones I loved to target! Even today if I was walking I can't lie. I would be Charles Bronson some people watch, some talk and some do things to fight fire with fire! I don't care for any one who punish torture innocent people and victimize them because they are defenseless! You Kill them! Why let them see your face!

Nonviolent these days my ink is deadlier then bullets shedding light on the people I mentioned all they need is a heat room and 72 hrs of questioning asking the correct questions is what get you what you need utilizing your pawns they are expandable! This is my purpose I been a target covertly for nearly 4 years while a combined crew of good guy, bad guys, work together to keep me silent of who I know? what I know!

I once sold drugs In Chicago, although I became a target, all for the wrong reasons. I wonder while going to court am I the bad guy? Or just a guy in the wrong place outnumbered by crooks in a disabled match in which they can't keep up with me? So they cheat and break the rules of the game and the blinded law! I have been law abiding 6 years to the day I stop walking and even defenseless! Although I fear no man even if he stands and threatened me I know about Life after death and death after Life, so how can they delete me, when after death they have to meet me? All the so called Gangster imitating Tony Montana, Scare face, Nino brown ole-dog and even Superfly.

I've seen time with life sentence destroy all crews and turn supermen into Super Dave! I've seen the hardest hood toughest, coldest bad, guys turn State evidence breaking the street code becoming Sammy the Bull after murdering 48 humans destroying even more life then after title telling the fear of being killed and murdered in Prison after they have snitched on all their best friends, to save their own lives. And to avoid prison now tell me if you live you should be able to receive it how you gave it. I don't fear death. I only fear cowards earning a stripe and cowards getting away with many crimes of defenseless old and innocently young people who are not responsible are in a case they shouldn't be victimized by cowards who will dukie in their pants if faced by the mirror effect of their persona deeds haunting them.

This is the message to J-hud this is connected and it ain't no stunt to gain wealth, it is my amends with God and my California street Credentials verification Spider G-unit knows my street codes how I ride and die by these rules of respect the Innocent guided the Ink while the voiceless spoke to me how this situation was worse then it has been played out as victims, they were torched as hostages the limit of time can be countless hours in attempts to obtain hundreds of thousands and the people who grew up getting so close to observe when to strike, Balfour wasn't alone tying down three people and a boy demanding money? This means killers continue to be at large the true killers! He may have kept his girl away knowing the nature of his co defendants who are free, his family may have become targets!

I write to set free the captured restless souls who are unhappy tormented at the very end of life unable to release feeling something is holding them back knowing your murderer walks in the light of life beyond death freely after ending innocent live beforehand before their time. I lay stiff in the alley 71 Stewart 45 minutes after being held at gun point caught gun less unable to throw rice grains, they shot men like me to earn stripes decorating the fear in the street polarized Kodak moments of who am I? Fear me! The attempt to even out do their co-defendants attempting to metamorph into the worse of the worse! Striking fear in even the next hood fella, so they shall never be challenged similar to the movie Juice with Tupac recognizing two individuals just from some sort of simple small talk, I heard them saying he saw your face, now he saw my face we gotta kill him! I knew they were establishing street names and their order was reckless. It got many killed, and many cowards a new heightened street name as they so-call added bodies to their profiles – most who have no gun – and become men who make threats until they are with Excalibur! Cowards without straps!

My purpose is illuminating these clowns and the crimes of senseless activities although committed cowardly by video gamers proving themselves while high and in a different approved drug state of thought, they carry out heinous crimes and this team is being dismantle all I need is modest Cops to begin with the first good guys who showed up during my near death moment. Figure out why so many finger prints on my truck vanished and if these dudes were arrested and convicted their maybe no J-huds family massacre discussion along with so many other quiet silent drug dealers who can't say much!   To the young boy justice will be served by God, my coming fourth or by law something will change to preserve someone's life!

About the Author & Book

The fourth book written by Raymoutez Price, **Life After Death, Death After Life: "The Arrival, The Awakening, The**

Departure" was published in July 2014 with the assistance of BePublished.Org in hopes of inspiring others who have faced traumatic situations and who have decided to never give up their will to live and simultaneously never fear facing death. After nearly losing his life several times, Ray found a purpose for existing that extended well beyond living for the sake of having life itself. This work, written while he was hospitalized for a life-threatening illness, shares Ray's thoughts on the worlds of spiritually and the rough realities of everyday life.

The author of **The Gang Capitol: The Art of Gang War and Racism Behind It** (2013), Raymoutez Price

penned **The Gang Capitol II: Crips In, Bloods Out** (2014) with the hope that its candid, thought-

provoking details will help promote peace and improve public knowledge, true understanding, and all communities. A father of seven, the Chicago resident is a native of the Watts area of Los Angeles and a former gang member who has changed his life, overcome many trials, and currently serves as a mentor to youth in both California and Illinois.

Mr. Price has endured the violence of both cities and has lost family members and friends in Los Angeles to the hands and brute force of senseless gang wars. He has lived in its grips of death and survived numerous attempts on his life. He was encouraged to pursue college which honed his ability to write and express his points of views. After the many attempts to figure out his story, the street life and his enduring tragedy, he finally got it after reading books by Tookie Williams and Monster Kody, and listening to so many countenance rap songs by Tupac and other rappers.

An example of forging forth in the face of harrowing circumstances, Mr. Price released this fourth labor of reflection at the same time he published his third literary project (**Game Of Pawns: "Game Is Told, Not Sold"**) during his extended hospitalization during July 2014. He credits his ability to move forward despite the odds to the African blood in his veins, 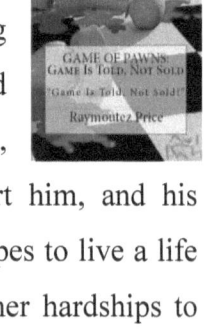 the love of his family and friends who support him, and his personal relationship with God. Mr. Price also hopes to live a life worthy to inspire others with disabilities and other hardships to never give up on fulfilling a dream, and to always work on completing goals no matter how many it takes to reach their success. His books are testaments to his legacy of continuing to fight and awaken street dwellers and those with slumbers of mind.